Oh My Soul!

**THE DEEP NATURE
OF AWARENESS**

*Personhood in
Christian Perspective*

Michael J Spyker

AgapeDeum

Published in Adelaide, Australia by AgapeDeum
Contact: agapedeum.com

ISBN

Copyright © Michael J Spyker 2022

All right reserved. Other than for the purpose and subject to the conditions prescribed under the *Copyright Act*, no part of this publication may be reproduced, stored in a retrieval system, or transmitted in any form or by any means, electronic, mechanical, photocopying, recording and otherwise, without prior permission of the publisher.

Publication assistance by Immortalise

Cover design: Ben Morton

CONTENT

Chapter 1	A Study of Soul	1
Chapter 2	A Unified Structure	8
Chapter 3	What Soul?	14
Chapter 4	Elegant Simplicity	20
Chapter 5	Presence	29
Chapter 6	Soul Awareness	39
Chapter 7	Demands of Soul Awareness	50
Chapter 8	Modes of Soul Awareness	58
Chapter 9	Place-making	65
Chapter 10	Soul Struggles	73
Chapter 11	Grounding the Soul	82
Chapter 12	A Deep Nature	91
Chapter 13	The Thinking Soul	99
Chapter 14	The Feeling Soul	109
Chapter 15	The Spirited Soul	122
Chapter 16	Oh My Soul!	131

1

A Study of Soul

For thousands of years philosophers and religious thinkers have written about the soul. Hardly surprising, for soul is what human experience is all about. Ideas have been plentiful and interesting. Historically, soul has been understood as immaterial, as spirit-like, until recently modern science and psychology joined the fray. They consider the concept of spirit outdated and soul a body manifestation. Scientifically, the phenomenon of soul is addressed in studies of the brain. Neurobiology is gaining considerable insights. The expectation is that one day brain function will reveal all.

The idea of people having a soul is readily accepted. Soul is central to a person's consciousness and every moment of awareness involves the soul. It reflects attitude, mind and emotions and is an indicator of wellbeing. It is no surprise that the reality of soul has been commented on throughout the ages. Aristotle had distinct ideas about it, as did St Augustine and other philosophers. Novelists have dealt with the nature of soul in many varied ways. These days the fields of biology, medicine and psychology are the new frontier.

Findings will remain limited when the dynamic of spirit is excluded. This view is held by many and not only by religious people. Life feels so much larger than merely being a body manifestation. Something else must be in play and it is called spirit. But what might the idea of spirit entail?

I hold that spirit is fundamental in how creation came about and is maintained. My book *Science and Spirit* (2020) is a study of spirit and matter, whereby matter is seen as a manifestation of spirit. God is Spirit. Creation issues from that Spirit and exists by it. As a thought experiment *Science and Spirit* offers a Christian response to scientific developments that declare anything of a spirit nature irrelevant.

The most amazing aspect of creation, however, was not discussed in this study. It fell outside of its scope. The reality of life, of enlivened matter, remained unaddressed. Even though the basic ideas used in *Science and Spirit* can be extended to offer insights on what it means to be alive. How the experiences called soul fit into creation's design.

Some ideas previously presented in *Science and Spirit* will be briefly restated in this present discussion and further developed to include dynamics of life. What is suggested will be both interesting and practical. About personhood recommendations are made towards the wellbeing of soul, with the Christian having the potential advantage of an enabling grace.

Apostle Paul declared that always we are looking into a mirror dimly when studying the workings of God (1Cor. 13:12). It is so with our heavenly future, as it is with inquiries into our world. An ultimate way in unveiling the mysteries of the universe does not exist. It is inherently impossible for people to achieve that. Recently, I wrote a parable called *Sepia Land* about human understanding and its limitations. It advocates a preferred approach when enquiring into those mysteries.

Sepia Land

In Sepia Land everything is brown. The wise woman sitting under a tree always was amazed at how much detail shades of brown could bring into the wide landscape before her. She knew of no other colour but brown. Mystics and Seers spoke of a Knowledge of Blue, a reality that was beyond Sepia Land. She was happy to accept their insights and felt what they talked about to be true.

But her brown eyes were incapable of seeing that Blue. It remained a mystery.

She reflected on how much the existence of Blue had become challenged, particularly of late. The materialists were investigating a Knowledge of Red and with great success, as was apparent in how fast technology had changed daily life. Materialists considered Blue to be an old-fashioned illusion. Scientific theories that delved into the immeasurable suggested the essence of Sepia Land to be Red. But brown eyes could never actually see Red, merely its manifestation.

People though are so much more than a physical reality, the wise woman reflected. What about feelings, intuition and imagination? How about morality and the ability of language? Yes, absolutely, there is a place for a Knowledge of Yellow, as philosophers had decided years ago. More recently, the human psyche had become subject to experiments by psychologists. These modern practitioners of Yellow now also viewed a Knowledge of Blue as a remnant of the past, the woman mused. Even though Yellow was a very deep phenomenon involving dynamics that in their origin escaped detection. Brown eyes were unable to see essential Yellow.

The wise woman enjoyed her brown world. She accepted that a Knowledge of Blue, Red and Yellow somehow were basic to it; that they were part of the unity of Sepia Land. She understood herself to be an interesting manifestation of those three primary colours, transformed together into another one. Her brown eyes lit up. Wasn't Sepia Land an interesting place!

*****

Placing the various disciplines of knowledge at loggerheads when seeking to understand God's universe is counterproductive. The natural sciences (Red) fighting the human ones (Yellow) for supremacy is not smart. Nor is it wise for religion (Blue) to mostly isolate itself. In this present study of the soul, the achievements in these fields of knowledge will be recognised. Personal preference always remains a factor when assessing information, while the manner in which insights by others are responded to is important. Differentiation is unavoidable but not so disharmony.

Might is be possible to create an understanding of existence that precedes this need for distinction into categories? An approach that considers reality at its most primary and unified form, from which the world, as it presents itself, is a derivative. Philosophy has undertaken this challenge a number of times. Most recently it was attempted by Alfred North Whitehead (1861-1947). For knowledge to become unified, Whitehead writes:

> 'It must be one of the motives of a complete cosmology, to construct a system of ideas which bring the aesthetic, moral, and religious interest into relation with those concepts of the world which have their origin in the natural sciences' (1929, vi).

This observation is relevant to a study of spirit, soul and body. Differentiated, but in relation, they always present as a unity of existence in creation. Whereby aesthetic, moral and religious understanding arises at the level of personhood. In Sepia Land the wise woman considered herself simply to be Brown, but as such, a manifestation of spirit (Blue), matter (Red) and soul (Yellow). This demarcation offers a way in which to study what being a person involves. It allows for an interpretation of God's unified handiwork in manageable terms.

The premise of *Oh My Soul!* is that *spirit* connects to divine reality with *body* being the material part of creation. *Soul* is an awareness that occurs because of the interplay between both. This model incorporates every aspect of how people experience life and can explain much. The approach taken will be biblical with insights from theology, philosophy and history. The natural sciences and psychology will also find a mention. The overriding purpose is to gain a better understanding of God's presence in personhood, in which opportunities towards wellbeing will be highlighted. Much in life involves making choices and becoming soul smart is one of those – a choice worth noting.

2

A Unified Structure

Thomas Merton wrote about Zen that, 'there is *nothing* which can be understood short of the basic demands of its structure' (1968, 1). Zen, as an expression of human experience, can be understood properly only when being aware of the construct of Zen and what it requires. This rule applies generally to all modes of understanding, including personhood. Insights are limited by how well the structure and demands of being human are recognised. In this, science, philosophy and psychology each come up short from a Christian perspective – the main reason being that the reality of spirit is ignored, while spirit is primary to the existence of our universe.

The natural sciences accept that most fundamentally all is energy. Quantum bits are energy manifestations. Spirit also is an 'energy' dynamic and the suggestion that the energy in our universe derives from spirit is philosophically reasonable. Quantum, in its more advanced deliberations, is solely based on pure mathematics with its reasoning ability and can never be empirically verified. It is a construct of ideas. Whether quantum or spirit, the deepest nature of all existence will remain a mystery. That quantum might be investigating manifestations of spirit is a distinct possibility.

The structure and demands of personhood are best considered in light of Scripture. In the realisation that earthly personhood is an image of the Personhood of God. Whereby the essence of my personhood involves the same functionality as the essence of God. For God cannot create but in accordance with the divine nature, of which the two most fundamental aspects it are Spirit and Love. All of creation is an expression of those two realities with the human being as the crown of God's achievements. This perspective was initially presented in my book *The Primacy of Love* (2015), how from spirit and love all originates. Briefly it reasons as follows.

God is Spirit. God's eternal Spirit created a universe that is holding together in that Spirit. The derivative manifestation of that Spirit in creation I have called *universal spirit.* There is no demarcation between eternal and universal spirit for God is One and undivided in everything. All of creation – its conceptualisation, energy, and reality – comes to exist by universal spirit, from quantum to personhood. The deepest dynamics of universal spirit are undetectable but its manifestations are not.

God is Love. Every act of God is an act of Love. In creation this eternal love manifests as *universal love*. It is the nature of universal spirit. Eternal love cannot separate from universal love, for it would deny what true love is about. God's Love always seeks to connect and is well able in doing so. In universal love the origins of life and the good are found. Its final manifestation, yet to come, will be eternal life and perfection.

Presently, God's creation is imperfect and struggles under the destructive influences of sin. Why an all-powerful God allows this to happen will forever be a mystery. A more pertinent question is, at which level of reality has sin entered creation? Blaming it on human behaviour misunderstands the intention of the Genesis story. Sin, as an agent of death, was active well before humans walked the earth. Sin is a force that affects all that exists, and always has for the influences of sin are imbedded into the very fabric of nature. This realisation places sin at the primary level of creation – the level of universal spirit and universal love, where love brings life and the good while sin brings death and evil. A logical assumption is that sin infiltrated universal spirit and love at the conception of creation. The unitive perfection of universal spirit and love carries a parasite.

This travesty Jesus came to undo by a self-giving act of love and mercy. Its magnitude is beyond our understanding. Sin is allowed to be active by God, but only for a season. The current creation is teleological - geared towards a preordained purpose of everlasting bliss. It seems that this perfected creation cannot be achieved without a sinful intermediate state, a mystery that remains with God.

The suggestion that creation finds it origin in universal spirit and universal love allows for a discussion of soul to become grounded into that structure of reality; with 'body' being a manifestation of universal spirit, while life is an expression of universal love. I consider soul to be the awareness that occurs in animate being because its body has become enlivened. At the level of personhood, this awareness reflects the very image of God. It brings to human experience a sense of what God is like. God may become understood and this awareness develops into conceptualisations and meaning.

There is *nothing* which can be understood short of the basic demands of its structure, Merton wrote. I suggest, that everything in creation is a manifestation of universal spirit and universal love, while God's handiwork is at one and undivided even though within it many unities of existence may be found. Personhood is such a unity with its basic structure of spirit, body and soul. Historically though, that tripartition has found varied receptions.

3

What Soul?

The word soul is a signifier that has meaning because of human experience. But of course that experience need not be called soul and isn't in different languages. It may not ellicit quite the same idea from one speaker to another either. More so, a given language may use different words referring to the same experience. That is so in English where soul and spirit are interchangeable depending on preference; when all the attributes of the soul are considered as residing in the spirit and vice versa. Whatever the word used, the experience refers to the feeling of being a body and simultaneously not a body – somehow separate from it in an extended way. As if the body is a vessel of the essential me. In English the word soul may even be used in reference to the whole person. Such as, 'she's a kind soul.' Soul, as an idea, is central to being human.

No wonder that so much has been written about it. A

brief exposé will never do it justice. Nevertheless, some mention of the history of 'soul' is helpful for that feeling of inner extension has a long past. Originally through religion followed by philosophy and these days by the sciences. Views and counterviews are many, as might be expected when engaging with the question of what 'being' is about. In the Western World, the most influential ideas were formulised in Greek civilisation hundreds of years before the days of Christ. Older ideas still, that are familiar to Western society, originated in the Middle East and became incorporated into the Old Testament.

A comprehensive exposition of biblical anthropology is given by writers Beck & Demarest. In the Old Testament the idea of soul (*nepes*) occurs 755 times and that of spirit (*ruah*) 378 times. But the usage of these words is flexible. A corresponding translation in English of *nepes* depends on context and varies. It may mean soul or life, signify the whole person, or heart and what we would call mind. While *ruah* is used for wind, physical breath, the Spirit of God and the life force of creatures (Beck & Demarest 2005, 130-132). In Old Testament times it was difficult to have the nature of being human neatly defined and that remains so today.

The idea that our immediate world exists in relation to an unseen mysterious one is as old as humanity; that earthly reality is connected and influenced by a superior one. Greek philosophy began to deliberate about the possible functionality of the transcendent. Its best known ideas are Plato's (*c.*425-347 BC) Realm of Being and Realm of Becoming, still relevant today. The Realm of Being is primary, the 'real reality'. It is non-substantial and contains perfect, everlasting Forms. The natural world of sense experience, the Realm of Becoming, is a shadow of that. A.C. Grayling explains how soul fits into Plato's thinking.

> We are not capable of inferring the existence of the Forms from their imperfect copies, given our delusive powers of perception and our finite intellects, therefore there must be another way we know them. This is that we have immortal souls which, while in their disembodied state before we are born, occupy the Realm of Being and are in direct contact with the Forms – and therefore, while in that state, we know everything (2019, 68-69).

Plato saw human intellectual capacity as possible because of 'memories' in the soul of a prior exalted existence.

Bodily function is rated lowly; a necessary imperfect vessel for the immortal soul. Aristotle (385-323 BC), a pupil of Plato, developed this understanding further. Instead of the Forms being an Idea separate from matter, they would be immanent in matter. Aristotle observed in his biological studies that nature is not static but continually progresses. It is dynamic and why would that be so? There must be a greater Cause making this happen. This Cause itself doesn't progress for then it would be part of nature, while by definition it is not. Thus, there exists an Unmoved Mover named God. This idea influenced theology a great deal and even today distorts our understanding of a Christian God who, in fact, is not remote and disengaged but immanent and active. People, animals and plants all have souls, Aristotle decided, each in accordance to their Forms.

This view of reality, and how it developed after Aristotle, influenced the writing of the New Testament. It never replaced God's revelation but helped with its interpretation. The Gospel of John begins with the Greek concept of Logos, 'the Word'. Unlike the synoptic gospels, John often mentions 'soul' in its narration. While Apostle Paul, once he became aware of the significant role of the Holy Spirit in peoples' lives, mostly refrained from using 'soul' in his letters in preference to 'spirit'. Though 1 Thessalonians 5:23 shows his recognition of the trichotomy spirit, soul and body in his wish for believers to be kept blameless in every aspect at the coming of Jesus, our Lord.

Paul followed Greek philosophy here, which held that personhood involved three facets: a body with its passions, soul in which reason, emotions and the will reside, plus an immortal spirit that relates to the transcendent. This demarcation allows for structured reflection on what being human is about. As a model it enables 'being' to be explained, which itself is indivisible. Not everyone agrees with this triple division though. Not today; nor from the Early Church onward.

Thomas Aquinas (1225-1274), that great theologian of the Middle Ages and well acquainted with Aristotle, preferred a dichotomy in considering the essence of personhood. 'Man is a single compound substance made of body and soul.... The human soul is a *spiritual* substance.... It is a substantial spiritual form. It is a spirit' (Glenn 1978, 60-61). Plato held that the soul is the actual person with the body merely a vessel. Not so, said Aquinas, the material and spirit side of being are of equal importance, singularly united.

More than 800 years earlier, St. Augustin (354-430) made use of Plato's ideas, but united spirit and soul in contrast to the body. People were rational souls living in material bodies. In this dichotomy, soul was the dominant term for the immaterial. Substance dualism has been the majority view of much of the Church through the ages. A person is considered one unity of being, an integration of material and immaterial. The immaterial side remains to exist after death. How to best explain that is still a much debated question.

Placing the emphasis on a unity of person, some thinkers prefer substance monism. It maintains that the reality of soul has not been proven. Therefore a person is a singular entity, a living body – no more, no less. This view interprets the Old Testament as being monistic. Dualism became introduced through the use of foreign philosophy, according to monists.

Modern science is monistic. A person simply is a body that lives. The idea of spirit is seen as illusionary for its existence cannot be scientifically verified. It is thus discarded with human experience being predominantly a matter of mind. The resulting mind/body problem is exclusively biological. Popular writer and reductionist Steve Pinker suggests the mind to be 'a neural computer, fitted by natural selection with combinatorial algorithms for causal and probabilistic reasoning about plants, animals, objects, and people' (1997, 524). Religion is just a trick of the mind, Pinker reckons. Understand the biological functions of the human body sufficiently and everything will be explained. If it cannot, it is because evolution is still in progress, as is our understanding.

But Pinker admits that consciousness and how people experience sensations remains a baffling problem to neurobiology. 'At least for now, we have no scientific purchase on the special extra ingredient that gives rise to sentience. As far as scientific explanation goes, it might as well not exists' (1997, 147).

The nature of soul remains scientifically elusive. Philosophy has frequently considered the enigma, while psychology developed many theories on its functionality. The question of 'What soul?' remains open, also from a Christian point of view, with further insights a possibility.

4

Elegant Simplicity

Life is a unity. Everything alive consists intrinsically of parts that cannot be separated and is either living or dead. Modern thinking doesn't cope well with the idea that in being alive, the material has been infused with the non-material. It is how Scripture presents life to be with spirit and matter somehow existing as a living unity. Science discards spirit as illusionary, while religion considers its reality essential. Science is one approach in understanding personhood. Intuition, supported by mystical insights, is another.

Science holds to the idea that the less complicated the answer to a problem, the greater is the possibility for that answer to be correct. It is called an elegant solution. This equally applies to considering the deep nature of life, that an elegant explanation of how creation functions, at its most primary, ideally will be simple. Such a simplicity will offer fundamentals whereby to address a complex phenomenon, using a few first principles.

Elegant Simplicity 21

As mentioned, these principles are: God is Spirit and God is Love. The nature of God's creative acts is spirit/love. Its manifestations are universal spirit and universal love, with God's handiwork being a unified whole, foundationally undifferentiated. Altogether, it is the structure by which the universe exists.

Every differentiation derives from a unified deeper level of reality. For instance, when universal spirit manifests as a living body, it is a unified expression of spirit and matter. When life departs, the body deteriorates. This deterioration occurs as an event within universal spirit as does the departure of the deceased entity's spirit. The spirit, in the form of its earthly body, returns to God in whom it has always existed. There is no dualism at the primary level, all is universal spirit. German scholar and theologian Franz Delitzsch (1813-1890) wrote that 'matter and spirit are only opposites relatively, not absolutely' (1969, 264).

Earthly experience however conditions me to see reality as a compilation of a multitude of different things. It is 'I' facing 'the other'; and so many of those in so many ways. An underlying unity of existence may be suggested, but is never really felt. Martin Buber tried to explain this with an 'I-Thou' concept, while admitting that the breakthrough into a unified vision of creation is rare indeed. If ever it happens, it will be brief. The mystics tell us that all is One, but how might this be formulised? For the One is divine, associated with a Greater Realm. In Hinduism that realm is beyond the gods. Buddhism, perhaps because the unity of One was sensed by the Buddha and this contradicted a diversity of all existence, does not have a concept of God (of an Other). Nor does it recognise a differentiated individual self within people. The very aim of Zen is to break through earthly reality into a unity of spiritual sight that surpasses all. A kaon is meant to overcome differentiation. Like, the sound of one hand clapping. It shatters dualistic perspectives.

In monotheism 'The (Wholly) Other' and the little human 'I' is central to religious understanding and is by nature dualistic. Jesus wished it differently though. He sought to cut through these limiting perceptions and found the best way forward in calling God, 'The Father.' The capable, caring and trustworthy Person you can get close to and feel at one with. Paul, understanding it well, encouraged believers to address God as Abba – Dad (Rom. 8:15). The very indwelling of God's Spirit suggests there to be no demarcation between Father and child, although using two nouns in mentioning it immediately suggest separation. Our thinking minds function in that

Elegant Simplicity 23

way for otherwise the world would be beyond understanding. But feeling-wise I am able to experience an immediacy between God and myself. That is the gift Jesus brings – his continual presence, united in spirit, with my soul feeling alive in a deeper reality. This spiritual differentiation, without demarcation, can be an everyday experience to those open to it.

It is hard to imagine non-dualistically. Ordinary thinking comes up short. It requires a special sense that is felt as true in spite of the protestations of pure reason. The mystics experienced it and found it difficult to verbalise what they saw. The dynamics of the Greater Reality can only be superficially explained. St John of the Cross wrote that a short time with God teaches you more than years of worldly instruction. 'More is gained in one hour from God's good things than in a whole lifetime from your own' (1991, 95). This may involve a being taken up in the spirit that is then later explained as a subject/object event. Imagination might seek to overcome this hurdle, but in the end it will fail. The experiences inferred by St John are uncommon. The ordinary Christian when sensing a familiarity with the Lord simply needs to accept the truth of that experience. This can translate into a sure knowing by faith, which may irk rationality. The mind though will have to follow the heart.

Delitzsch wrote that, 'matter and spirit are only opposites relatively, not absolutely.' They are two manifestations of a common denominator. Connecting a spirit reality to an earthly one has a long history in which Plato and Aristotle remain significant. The suggestion that perfect Form or Idea is the origin of an imperfect natural world has never quite left philosophical thought. It has also been much used in theology.

Theology has associated Plato's concept of 'Idea' with the 'Mind' of God. Two Christian philosophers did develop this understanding in a similar way. They were known to each other, though the first gave little encouragement to the second. Both made the mind of God central in thinking about existence – God's power of reason, imagination and ability to create accordingly. The first philosopher was Spinoza and the second Leibniz. They are of interest because the concept of universal spirit partially aligns with their ideas. Both were influenced by the Neoplatonic principles that mind is more fundamental than matter and that the ultimate cause (originator) of all things must be a single unitary principle (Grayling 2019, 124).

In his book *Ethics*, Benedict Spinoza (1632-77) writes

extensively about the nature and origin of human mental ability. It originates from within the mind of God. God has ideas and actualises them into a finite creation. 'For of everything there necessarily exits in God an idea of which He is the cause' (2001, 57). God's ideas are perfect and complete, although creation is not. Mind, which equates with reason, makes the natural world come about. Within that world, mind is of the highest value, while the body also expresses the essence of God, as all else does (2001, 45). In both a person's mind and body God is immanently present. They 'are the very same thing' (Kenny 2010, 671). The mind is purely reason and has no understanding of (affinity with) the passions of the body. These passions are to be intellectually assessed however and evaluated as to their prudence with, if necessary, the mind taking control over emotions. Spinoza summed up the soul as the idea of the body. 'What this means is not obvious, but it is at least clear that Spinoza thinks that in order to understand the soul we have to first understand the body' (Kenny 2010, 671). Perhaps Spinoza assumed that sentience resides in the body in accordance with God's prescriptive Idea. The resulting dynamic is called soul in which free will, according to Spinoza, does not exist. All is inescapably causal and the result of what God sets in motion. Everything, existence and motion in their smallest detail, emanates from God's mind and activity.

Gottfried Wilhelm Leibniz (1646-1716) 'was one of the supreme intellects of all time, but as a human being he was not admirable,' Bertrand Russell writes (1996, 531). Leibniz took issue with the idea that matter was an extension (separate) of mind, as had been suggested by René Descartes (1596-1650), who wrote '…. God created a rational soul, and joined it to this body in a particular way…' (1988, 65), referring to the human body. Leibniz was aware of Descartes' philosophy, but held that in God mind and body are essentially the same thing. In explaining how creation might originate, he envisaged an entity in God's mind that was primary before all else. Through this entity, which is non-substantial and like a thought, creation comes about; when God decides to explicitly activate an entity rather than annihilate it. A. C. Grayling explains that it is 'a mind-like entity, "simple" in the logical sense of being "non-complex", and the most fundamental thing there is' (2019, 237). Leibniz called these simple entities 'monads'. They are dynamic and 'ensouled'.

Leibniz designed an extensive philosophical construct explaining our reality. How monads, their number uncountable and endless, work in shaping creation.

Elegant Simplicity 27

Monads have no knowledge of each other and each 'mirrors' a whole world in itself. As such they are not in relation, which as an idea is confusing. In his cosmology Alfred North Whitehead (1861-1947), aware of Leibniz's achievements, replaced monads with 'actual entities or occasions of experience.' Rather than being individual, those occasions are interrelated.

The ideas of Spinoza, Leibniz and Whitehead are far too briefly presented here to do their thinking justice. It merely is to show that great minds have seen it fit to search for a simple idea behind the complexity of creation. That viewpoint remains relevant. As scientific knowledge progresses, it has become clear that from the very small, the large comes forth. The basic laws of deep space are but a few. A single theory, which is wave theory, offers insights about what is happening many lightyears away. While in our natural world much is determined by solely DNA and genes. These carriers of information are extremely small, but what they make happen can be quite enormous. The thought that creation originates from a still deeper reality that somehow acts upon quantum particles to bring about our reality, is not foreign to scientific reflection. But how to conceptualise that reality is unknown. A secret with to what is known as 'God'.

The depths of God's mind are inscrutable. Its creative power cannot be penetrated. Whatever may be known on earth comes from God's self-revealing and from people existing in the image of God making sense of their reality. All knowledge is based on the human ability of creative interpretation. Insights that range from reaching out into primary reality right up to lived experience. One way of obtaining such knowledge philosophically is the use of spirit, soul and body as interpretive concepts. It is elegant in its simplicity.

5

Presence

The material world is readily recognisable but not so that of spirit and soul, which are subjective qualities. Historically, the usage of the words spirit and soul has been considered interchangeable depending on one's preference. In reflecting on animate life a differentiation between spirit and soul is helpful. Whereby soul is an awareness that results from the interaction between spirit and body.

Genesis 2:7 reveals that God formed the person from matter and by the breath of God's Spirit, Adam became a living being. Delitzsch writes extensively on this. How the infusion of body with spirit created soul, which is the interplay between body and spirit. 'Man is henceforth a living soul by the power of the spirit of life, wherewith God has endowed him' (1966, 253). The soul has a foot in both camps, so to speak. Ecclesiastes 12:7 states that upon death 'the dust returns to the earth as it was, and the spirit returns to God who gave it.' Whether the idea of soul was ever in the mind of whoever wrote this, at death the breath of earthly life is no more and thus, following the model under discussion, the living soul has vanished.

Visionary, naturalist and musician Hildegard of Bingen (1098-1179) explained:

> A human being contains three paths: namely, soul, body and senses. On these three paths human life runs its course. The soul fills the body with life and brings forth the senses; for its part the body attracts the soul to it and opens the senses; in turn the senses touch the body and draw the soul to them(2001, 7).

This appears to have been the common understanding in medieval days. Had Hildegard used the terms body, soul and spirit, then in her explanation the word soul would have been replaced by spirit and senses with soul. The dynamics she alluded to remain recognised also today.

Defining soul as awareness of being is non-problematic and fits with how human existence is understood. It matters little where that awareness is thought to find its sense. What does matter are the corresponding feelings and experiences. Theology may suggest that essentially soul is spirit. Fine, it doesn't alter the awareness. Science will consider it a body dynamic. Also fine, life feels just the same. Soul is yet being investigated even though its existence is ignored. While not accepting soul being an awareness that originates from the interplay between spirit and body as a concept, psychology may yet gain insights that, where suitable, should be used in Christian understanding. Philosophy took the liberty to speculate widely about what soul entailed and offers suggestions.

Aristotle stretched the idea of soul beyond what is commonly accepted. When matter becomes organic it results in soul, he decided. Kenny explains,

> The soul's very essence is defined by its relationship to an organic structure. Not only human, but beasts and plants have souls ……. intrinsic principles of animal and vegetable life (2010, 192).

Defining soul as awareness sets narrower boundaries, whereby the level of awareness will depend on the nature of its living entity. That of animate life we can observe. That of people, we are inescapably familiar with.

What causes matter to become organic Aristotle never said. Nor has modern science found the primary reason for it. The deep influences that are guiding the universe remain a mystery.

Theologian and scientist John Polkinghorne refers to these influences as 'information' from the hand of God. While theologian Wolfhart Pannenberg suggested that the Holy Spirit might be a Field; in reference to field theory in physics. What I have called universal spirit is unlikely to be a field, but it does carry information and spreads out everywhere. In other words: it is ever present.

Besides being ever present, the 'information' in universal spirit is also ever active. For theoretical purposes I will call that ever present source of information and activity, 'Presence.'

Though universal spirit and Presence are inseparable, a differentiation is helpful. The feelings elicited when using concepts can differ. Some words represent a general idea not suggesting a particular. They are kind of vague. Presence is such a word, unlike the word spirit which commonly is understood to represents a sense of being. When contrasting spirit and matter both signify a particular, while the idea of Presence is non-particular in every way, apart from alluding to a relational quality. I suggest that in Presence the reality of all creation is contained, as it exists in the Person of Jesus Christ

(Col.1:15). Our universe rests in the embrace of an ever present and engaged God.

Presence, as a concept related to God, is not a new idea. Martin Buber in *I and Thou* used it in reference to divine interactions which people receive. 'Man receives, and receives not a specific "content" but a Presence, a Presence as power' (1958, 110). Buber uses the word Presence in describing a relational dynamic.

What however does Presence entail in how I would like to use the concept? Its essence is a divine unity from which, at God's command, diversity issues as a created realm. Presence is neither material nor a field, as in field theory. Modern physics suspects some dynamic to be the primary source of everything that exists. Presence is that source which, somehow, translates into forces that hold the universe together. The 'information' issuing from Presence at quantum levels is instrumental in bringing about cosmic forces and matter. That matter may become enlivened and even animate. At its most advanced level it presents a moral quality and then is called a person. The information needed for all this is contained in Presence and the resulting dynamics, from the infinitesimal minuteness of quantum to the very large power fields of the cosmos, derive from it. Presence is the database and primary energy of our universe.

This theory of existence may be further explained as follows. The full potential of creation, its history thus far and future to come, resides in Presence. Presence is the origin of every possibility and a record of the universe over time. Every manifestation in creation is a realised potential from within Presence. It guides the stars and keeps the black holes sucking them up. Every manifestation taps into the potential of Presence in accordance with its design, which itself originates from Presence. Inert matter simply is as it is. A fish will by design access the information in Presence differently from a bird. A horse will be a horse for its being carries the information of a horse and it lives accordingly. DNA, the building blocks of Presence for entities that involve growth, both enables a horse and restricts it. A horse can run but not fly. It can neigh but not sing. In its reality as 'horse' it *is* Presence. All the possibilities of the universe reside in Presence, but a manifestation or entity can only realise its Presence potential in accordance with the capacities inherent in its original design.

Creation evolves over time. Its progression is known to God while developments occur within existential categories – manifestations of a similar kind. Vegetation is such a category, as are reptiles. God may intervene directly in the development of a category, or create a new one. But the most common change within a category occurs due to environmental pressures and adaption over time. It involves chance and choice, both of which are central to the functioning of creation within the parameters set by God.

The human person, as a single entity, accesses a great amount of information from Presence. Personhood is the crown of what Presence ultimately makes possible. It begins at conception, continues until death and beyond. Delitzsch writes, 'with the embryonic beginning of bodily life is produced, at the same time, the beginning of the spirit's and soul's life' (1966, 254).

At every instant of growth, Presence enables Form to become realised through universal spirit. For living entities the blueprint of that Form is contained in its DNA and genes. As Delitzsch explains about people, which equally applies to lesser creatures: 'Spirit and matter are combined into a personal unity, by means of which the spirit not only is brought under the law of natural development, but also is in many ways conditioned by matter' (Delitzsch 1966, 262).

A full development of the Form's blueprint is not

guaranteed. It depends on the quality of its 'seed' and whether situational factors are favourable towards growth or otherwise. Creation shows that many entities never reach their full potential. Presence will not intervene in these natural processes, unless God decides otherwise.

Body and spirit are a unity of existence that as an entity can avail itself of information in Presence corresponding with its matter/body design. For that reason a fish is a fish and a person cannot communicate like a bat. By nature, personhood is restrictively human with the unique ability of moral choice. Only people have this capacity, and only after a certain age. Immanuel Kant (1724-1804) distinguished between *a priori* knowledge (independent of experience) and *a posteriori* (after experience). I know by nature (*a priori*) the good from the bad, though that is cultural also. While I know what love is like, because I have experienced love (*a posteriori*).

God creates in accordance with the divine nature, a nature that is fully encapsulated in Presence. On earth it manifests to the extent that bodily structure allows for it. A tree will not experience love; or at least we are not aware that it does. Animal species do know love, as for instance bird life shows. It may be assumed that for people the experience of love is more nuanced. Love is the nature of God.

God's nature is likewise endowed with the ability of making choices, which in the human being culminates in moral capacity. It concerns possibilities of value, which reside in Presence and reflect God. The potential of any life, realised or not, is by definition *a priori*. How well spirit and body are able to develop in tandem towards reaching a given potential in accordance with its perfect Form depends on inherited factors, opportunity and existential exposure. How life is experienced, will always be *a posteriori*, as Kant stipulated – for all creatures.

In the unity of spirit and body, spirit identity and body identity are one and the same. But when a living entity dies, the body disintegrates. Not so spirit, which in keeping its form and identity, encloses the full record of the life that was lived. With people that is biblically clear, for how can God hold the dead to account personally unless the experiences and memories of their life on earth remain? It seems consistent to assume that when one day the whole of creation will be liberated into the eternal Presence of God (Rom. 8:21), it will also have its perfect Form realised without blemish in the New Creation.

Presence contains the possibility of the perfect and is teleological. Currently its information has become contaminated within creation by sin. However, the victory of Christ over sin now makes the realisation of the perfect possible. One day, Presence will present its ultimate expression in the realm of the New Creation, where all will be without the damages of sin and true to its perfect Form. It means that any malfunction and disability will disappear, with everything functioning as designed by God before sin got a foothold. Centuries ago, medieval mystic Lady Julian of Norwich (1342-c. – 1423) in her visions saw the happening of a special day, when God will do a great deed and make all things well (1978, 232-233).

6

Soul Awareness

Human awareness is complex and in addressing it the use of a model facilitates clarity; even though what is being investigated is far more diverse than a model can fully explain. The idea of spirit, soul and body helps reflect on the integrated unity of personhood, a unity that will dissolve only in death. Human experience is indivisible but different aspects of it may be recognised, like having that sense of being more than just a body; the notion of consciousness and a perception of depth within the psyche that feels mysterious. Personhood is a multi-levelled reality that presents in singular moments of experience.

When I have a toothache my whole being becomes involved. My sore tooth is a body problem that affects my spirit. The resulting feeling is soul awareness, which helps me make sense of my world –what is happening to me. I walk in the dark and become fearful in spirit. My body begins to sweat and my awareness sharpens. All this I experience simultaneously. In deciding to take heart my spirit strengthens and, if needed, I will make my body run. It is a whole of person event in which I feel singularly focused. But when later I seek to explain in more details what was happening within me that singularity divides into a number of dynamics that involve personhood.

The categories of spirit, body and soul lend themselves well to explaining life. By including the idea of soul instead of merely a spirit/body concept, it allows for a demarcation between the immediacy of experience, what I am aware of, and that of the subconscious, which belongs to the realm of spirit.

I spend my days in soul awareness. It can occur even during my dreaming when asleep, in moments when I am able to decide, 'this is a dream, who cares?' and snap out of it. Or, when in the morning, I remember a dream. Soul is awareness of whatever I sense to be happening to me. Much about me, I know nothing of, both physically (all the bugs in my stomach) and in spirit (my deeper reality). How I experience myself, and in whatever situation, that is soul.

Soul is awareness supported by deeper being, a depth that as spirit interacts with my body. As spirit, by means of universal spirit, it also connects with Presence. My experiences of soul occur within Presence, as is the case for whatever happens to all that has life. Soul is the unitive inter-existence of spirit and body expressed at the level of consciousness for all that is so capacitated. At the level of personhood, this awareness is infused with the knowledge of good and bad and I am capable of love and sin the most destructive of which is called evil.

Though imperfect, the soul is never cut off from God. Creation in every detail is an expression of the divine Self and any act of God inescapably exists in God, for God cannot be extended beyond. However troubled nature might be, sin cannot ever alienate God from it and quite the reverse. The Son of God lived in our world completely associating with all that human life entails – divinity incarnate.

Creation is not pre-scripted and has freedom to develop within its categories. From the information residing in Presence every entity will seek to maximise its possibilities in accordance with its God given design. Full potential will often not be reached, not because God determines it so, but due to situational difficulties. God offers potential without absolute certainty.

For personhood it includes the question of free will: the choices made during a life. Spinoza concluded that everything, in its minutest details, occurs exclusively because of God's direct involvement and is inescapable. This philosophical approach makes free will an illusion and does not ring true to human experience for choice is an obvious dynamic in nature. Whatever has intelligence, is free to make choices. With personhood it becomes a moral capacity that allows for spontaneity. The notion that spontaneity would be fully scripted by God, seems a contradiction in terms. While morality is without intrinsic value if occurring under God's direct control. There is a difference between God's foreknowledge and whether God directs events thus beforehand. Foreknowledge does not exclude the existence of free will.

With choice being part of creation, its teleological advancement has to be unscripted – to a point. Like a river that flows within its banks. It is clearly guided both in its limitations and its destination. But water molecules move freely depending on flow, turbulence and the weather. Likewise, universal spirit is filled with the possibilities in Presence that become actualised as matter, and may contain the option of a response that determines how those manifestations of matter interact. In this manner creation moves on. Like the weather affects the river, God can intervene into the dynamic process when considered necessary and does, but the river will flow. Universal spirit unerringly moves forward towards its destination: a magnificent creation with a great history, and it will last forever.

The incredible potential in Presence is most significantly realised in the human being. What sets people apart is that in their bodily design they can replicate God's attributes better than any other creature. The Genesis story bears this out. God breathed the divine breath into Adam's nostrils and he became a living soul. In making personhood a reality God did the actual breathing in but not so with the rest of creation. It signifies that the nature of the spirit thus imparted has qualities resembling the divine to a significant extent. Spirit and body together are able to demonstrate God's abilities. At a much reduced level, but like God all the same.

In people, soul awareness is a reflection of God's nature though marred by sin. The potential available to people from Presence is a god-likeness and the level at which this will be realised depends on disposition – the manner in which choices are made during a life. God knows all and is able to evaluate the quality of someone's life in light of choice and circumstance. God cares and is merciful.

This god-like potential of personhood was confirmed by Jesus who, when the Jews accused him of calling himself God, retorted that in their own law people are called gods (Psalm 82:6), so surely the Son of God could use that qualification for himself. That the Son of God became a human being, and that even being possible, shows how closely personhood resembles God. Jesus was one of us, and in a divine way still is, but as a renewed Person, who resides as King of Kings in Heaven; the first of many people likewise to be so renewed. Personhood exhibits godly qualities and it will do so eternally.

The capacities of personhood mirror the attributes of God. God has a will, and so do people. God thinks, creates and feels and people do likewise. God plans and God remembers. Every essential capacity of what makes a person is found in God. The animal world and its abilities also derives from God. Its reality, like all else, originates from Presence, which is the dynamic totality of God's creative design.

Soul awareness is whatever a person (or living entity) experiences when spirit/body interaction reaches the level of consciousness. The full potential of human actualisation on earth only Jesus Christ could realise as his physical and spirit abilities would have been capable for that. The powerful influences of sin tried to prevent it. Not at the level where sin has infiltrated the material, for Jesus would have died a natural death had the cross not intervened. He was subject to the forces of nature like any other person. It was in his spirit that Jesus needed to remain sinless for a perfected future of creation to become possible. In his spirit, Jesus would have struggled greatly being aware of the pitfalls leading to failure; a challenge that would have translated acutely into his soul awareness.

Jesus succeeded facing incredible odds and after his death Presence welcomed someone born of the earth who was perfect in spirit; a person without the marks of sin from a worldly existence, even though in Jesus' dying God allowed the full weight of sin to bear upon him. In human form, Jesus expressed God's nature faultlessly. He absorbed sin by the power of love, made it powerless and placed it legitimately under God's control. This self-giving act introduced a very different dimension into Presence's potential – the possibility of a New Creation free of sin.

Human soul awareness replicates the attributes of God. Sin brings dynamics in play that are not anything like God. It does so as a parasitic spoiler, is not part of the primary source of nature's possibilities, and degrades human ability with its many modes of expression, the major ones being: will, thought, memory, affectivity and morality. The question arises, particularly these days with the sciences investigating the brain extensively, where these abilities reside in personhood. Science seeks to find their origin in the material. For a Christian, the question is one of spirit/body, with personhood understood as being non-dualistic.

Searching for the 'place' within personhood of qualities like morality or wisdom is futile. They are possible because of how the living human body is functionally designed with every ability an interplay between spirit and body. Those abilities are open to investigation for a better understanding. Undoubtedly, brain function determines much, but so does a person's spirit reaching into Presence. The origin of human ability is divine and will remain impenetrable.

Historically, inquiries into personhood have placed certain abilities above others and have explained soul awareness accordingly. Greek philosophy valued thought above all else. Two millennia later, René Descartes famous statement, 'I think therefore I am,' confirmed it for a modern world that treasures reason. The idea of thoughts superiority has infiltrated theology as well. Its presentations can become overly 'reasonable' and the gospel does not escape this tendency. The mind is important, which the New Testament often confirms. However, as A.W. Tozer warns, 'the gospel is addressed not to reason but to faith' (1978, 97). German theologian and mystic Meister Eckhart (c. 1260-1329), for all his learning and love of it, began to value intuition as the most profitable way of interacting meaningfully with God. 'Recognising the divine in oneself, and the universe, offered Eckhart a direct experience of God that was much more satisfying than any rational model' (Harrington, 2018, 162). Within God's being, divine qualities are not graded as to their significance and neither should that happen with regard to people. Every ability is equally important, whether reason or the intuitive, and ignoring this fact presents a stunted view of personhood.

Another human capacity present in the soul that has found prominence in philosophy from ancient days onward is the idea of 'the will'. The ability to make choices wilfully is a major component in how life may be lived. Both Aristotle and Augustine imagined the will as an issuer of commands, that may either be obeyed or not. It is considered an influence of significant force. These prominent thinkers took a special interest in what it meant to manage the will, for better or worse.

More recently, philosopher Arthur Schopenhauer (1788-1860) elevated the concept of will to a level that reaches beyond human ability. He made will synonymous with what I have called universal spirit and perceived it as a forward moving dynamic behind earthly realities. Much impressed with Buddhism, Schopenhauer left the idea of God out of his reasoning. For him, 'Will is the noumenal reality underlying all appearances, and therefore the whole of nature,' Grayling explains. 'We experience will directly, intimately, within ourselves; it predates conscious knowledge, and is completely separate from it' (2019, 299). In Kantian terms, the will is thus essentially *a priori*. Schopenhauer would have used the concept of will not finding a better way in which to define the force behind everything that his philosophy was referring to. In his day he became a celebrated dignitary. His is not, of course, how the idea of will is generally understood.

Soul awareness in people involves significant abilities and a myriad of experiences and thus raises many questions. Why do I have emotions? Where do they come from? And, how about memory, is that just a brain function? Not to mention that I seem to know the difference between good and evil almost naturally. And where does 'mind' fit within all this? The secret to all these questions hides in spirit/body unity. There is no one particular place for these modes of awareness within personhood.

In this unity, the brain cannot enable a person without the help of spirit. While the expressions of spirit are limited by the capacities of the brain, and not just the brain, but the body overall determines the abilities and limits of spirit expression in everything that lives. For every entity the perfect Form resides in Presence and will appear in its perfection in the New Creation. During this earthly existence when body/spirit dynamics manifest as awareness, it is called 'soul'.

This model offers a Christian perspective on our universe, and that of personhood in particular. Living out the image of God on earth however requires more than placing human experience within a conceptual framework. There are principles to be understood, that will guide the soul safely in a sea of change.

7

Demands of Soul Awareness

Thomas Merton wrote that 'there is *nothing* which can be understood short of the basic demands of its structure.' For soul that structure is awareness experienced due to the interaction of spirit and body. But what might be the basic demands of soul? Such demands would be foundational to human experience, in the sense that they are unavoidable and shape awareness at a deeper level while inescapably influencing the reality of personhood.

I suggest there to be four soul demands that must find their proper expression for life to become well lived. Those demands apply to life in general and are readily understood. The first is *belonging* and the second *becoming*. Together they comprise the more passive side of soul awareness. The active side includes *turning* and *relating*. These four dynamics involve relationality and as such correspond to the nature of our universe in which everything exists in relation. Their psycho-spiritual functionality will be discussed later. Presently, I like to show how readily the four concepts are used in everyday communication and meta-messages.

I received a letter some weeks ago from my health fund in response to the COVID 19 challenges. I need not worry for I *belong* to a healthcare family that cares and got me covered. The fund would not administer their intended fee increase, yet. The letter used the most important aspect of soul wellbeing, that of belonging, in the hope that I, feeling part of their 'family', would be grateful enough not to cancel my health cover. In society the word 'family' describes the idea of belonging best, which is often alluded to also in a club environment.

For a club to become truly meaningful to a person all four demands of the soul must be attended to. Many clubs these days, or even a whole sports, present themselves as a family – e.g. the football family. It engenders that sense of *belonging* better than most. Either, because I come from a good family, or if not, I would be looking for one and that is what the club offers. Signing up for membership will help me develop (*becoming*) into a real supporter. I may legitimately tap into the club's history as an identity enhancer.

But club membership has its demands. I am expected to *turn* my hand towards matters to be looked after and my wallet towards the club's financial needs. I must be interactive and *relate* with fellow supporters. Then that sense of real *belonging* will become strengthened. The basic demands resident within the structure of my soul now have been addressed and moved full circle: *belonging, becoming, turning* and *relating*; which then enhances *belonging* and another circle of relational experiences begins. My deep-seated needs are being met and this can be helpful towards wellbeing. There is nothing wrong with enjoying a club environment apart from a feeling perhaps that the concept of family is stretched a little far.

Church has followed suit. There are many who call themselves *Family* church thus suggesting it to be a place for the whole family and together a church family. If it satisfies the four basic demands of the soul well, it will be a good church, as God intended it relationally to be.

Unfortunately, whether church or club, creating a unified sense of belonging is far from easy. There tend to be strong egos and many ideas within a congregation of people. Disharmony often develops and the dynamics of healthy being then are violated. It becomes extra serious when that sense of belonging diminishes. Belonging is the cornerstone of the four basic demands of the soul and its importance cannot be stressed enough.

Swiss physician Paul Tournier (1898-1986) records how he sat together with a deeply troubled young man with whom he had formed a friendship.

> He was sitting by my fireside, telling me of his difficulties, of the anxiety that never left him, and which at times turned to panic and to flight. He was trying to look objectively at what was going on inside himself and to understand it. Then, as if summing up his thought, he looked at me and said: "Basically, I'm always looking for a place – for somewhere to be" (1968, 9).

A place to be. A significant place in which to belong. That sense of really belonging, which is essential to wellbeing, instead of being adrift; of not feeling anchored deep within your soul and the insecurities that brings. It is a problem faced by many and a difficulty not readily overcome. Belonging is the rock of life. Tournier's book *A Place for You* is a valuable read. The idea of place-making will be further commented on in a late chapter.

Everyone feels a measure of estrangement deep within as philosopher and theologian Paul Tillich (1886-1965) so accurately noted. It is the effect of sin marring Presence at the primary level of existence and working itself out in creation. Love unites – sin divides. Jesus came to undo this aberration and his victory changed everything. Not that God was ever estranged from creation. God's love always connects and remains fully active. Love bears all things, as Apostle Paul wrote (1Cor. 13:4-7). Not yet, but in the New Creation everything will belong in a perfect place unrestrictedly enjoying God's love. God has never limited that love, but the dynamics of sin obscure it. In Christ, God has broken down every wall for those willing to believe that divine love is fully accessible.

About this New Reality, in which sin has been defeated, theologian Karl Rahner writes:

> The new creation has already started, the new power of a transfigured earth is already being formed from the world's innermost heart, into which Christ descended by dying. Futility, sin and death are already conquered in the innermost realm of all reality (1964, 92).

This fundamental change in creation cannot be naturally detected. It is a matter of faith. Whether I believe in it or not changes nothing about the New Reality as such. But in accepting the truth of this change that is happening 'in the innermost realm of all reality' (as Rahner called it), I will be changed personally. I need now no longer feel estranged within a massive universe. For I belong with God, the creator of it all. Paul called this altered state of being, a justification 'by faith' (Rom. 3:28). The change thus secured within me becomes a felt certainty over time when in my soul there is a new kind of awareness. Applying faith persistently will strengthen my sense of divine belonging, which in turn strengthens my faith. By sticking firmly to this positive soul dynamic, I can build my life on rock instead of drifting sand.

Our world is laden with rejected and disenfranchised people who feel they do not belong. It is the most difficult, negative feeling for soul awareness to deal with. The shipwrecks are plentiful and continuing. Children, who experience parental alienation, carry a wound within them for the rest of their lives. It may result in coping behaviours that badly limit the joys of life. Why is it that those who are adopted yearn to find their original parents? Having been abandoned does that to the soul. Not to mention the many people around the globe who feel abandoned and may have been displaced from home and hearth.

The young student said to Paul Tournier, 'I'm always looking for a place.' Being from a rich home he was well cared for but exposed to absentee parenting. He lacked that sense of real belonging, which built up an emotional blockage and was limiting his social adaption. Tournier detected a kind of law in human wellbeing. 'He who has once experienced of belonging in a place, always finds a place for himself afterwards; whereas he who has been deprived of it, searches everywhere in vain' (1968, 12). Paul Tournier understood that the lack of a place in which the soul feels it belongs, inhibits the ability to achieve personal relationships.

The soul's need of belonging is a direct reflection of what is most important about God. Whatever else may be said about the divine attributes, the nature of God is love. Love cares and embraces. Love cannot but offer a deep sense of true acceptance. A sense of safety and enablement. Love builds one up. It is the fundamental life giving force within Presence. The human spirit yearns for it and thrives by it. Love seeks to connect, whereby the feeling of belonging to God arises from an act of faith that translates into a conviction of its veracity.

In my Father's house are many rooms,' Jesus said. 'If it were not so, would I have told you that I go to prepare a place for you?' Jesus is a place-maker. Not from a distance, but close by. 'And when I go and prepare a place for you,' he continued, 'I will come again and will take you to myself, that where I am you may be also' (John 14: 2-3). Jesus has taken the world into his heart and there is no better place.

'I am always looking for a place,' the young man told doctor Tournier. A place in which the four basic demands of the soul's structure are being met. It is a deep need common to all. In a world that is adrift, the Christian does well in remembering this.

8

Modes of Soul Awareness

On a clear night in the Australian desert the sky is amazing filled with a myriad of stars. The haze of light across the heavens is so astounding that thoughts remain in abeyance. It is a marvellous experience, one King David had many years ago. Seeing all the splendour, he wondered why God would bother with someone as small and fragile as a person. 'But you have made him a little less than God and crowned him with glory and honour,' David concluded (Psalm 8:3-5). In his spirit he would have felt the truth of that.

People are sufficiently what God is like that God could become a person. Jesus, who was in the form of God, emptied himself to become a servant to humankind (Phil. 2:6-8). This stepping away from his majesty placed him within the limits of earthly personhood, but it did not change his godly nature, which remained in human form and was crucial to the task ahead. Every person carries God's image even though it is hampered by sin. Soul awareness reflects God's attributes, at least to an extent, but in a damaged way. Awareness involves a multitude of experiences none of those foreign to God. Even the ravages of sin are known to the Father through the Son Jesus Christ, whose divinity would have carried his earthly experiences into the Godhead – the challenges of moral choice and sufferings in countering the power of sin.

The soul has many abilities physiology seeks to explain mostly from studies of the brain for it is central to consciousness. The brain responds to all stimuli from the body and the five senses and neurobiology increasingly begins to understand how that functions. It is to be admired. However, many scientists concede that major questions remain unanswered and probably always will be. The reductionist view, that everything is a manifestation of matter, is popular only in certain scientific quarters and surely foreign to Christian deliberations. Nevertheless, how do human abilities come to be and what determines their development?

Philosopher John Locke (1632-1704), borrowing from Aristotle, had an answer to the latter question. He suggested that people are born as a blank slate. It was based on the notion that in human development environmental exposure is instrumental. The experiences of life and one's responses determine all. The human mind is malleable, like a plain sheet of paper to be written on, and that writing can be conditioned.

In psychology this led to the theory of behaviourism, the study of how to shape behaviour by showing its consequences, or creating those. For a long time it was influential. These days behaviourism has lost its lustre. In his book *The Blank Slate* (2002) Steve Pinker points out that gene studies have shown behaviourism to come up short as genes have an influence on what a person is like. Hereditary traits readily verify the truth of that. But there is a limit to how much is defined by genes. They entail a probability and are not deterministic. People will make their choices in life according to preferences.

So, how then do human abilities come to be? The information carried in a person's genes to a great extent decides on what that individual can be like. This is strictly a body phenomenon. Physicality in itself though is insufficient in deciding personhood. In a living entity, body is never devoid of spirit. Apart from genes, spirit is the other source of an information that is derived from Presence. The influences of spirit are both shaped by gene potential and will enlarge it. In Presence all of reality exist in a relation that is ever active, some of it humanly noticeable though little understood. The concept of a collective unconscious by Carl Jung, which he considered common to all, is an example. He tells how one night it seemed that someone was visiting him after being awakened 'by feeling a dull pain, as though something had struck my forehead and then the back of my skull. The following day I received a telegram saying that my patient has committed suicide. He had shot himself. Later, I learned that the bullet had come to rest in the back wall of the skull' (1989, 137-138). There is much more to reality than what genes make possible.

Human ability is very multifaceted and loosely may be clustered into four modes of awareness. People can *think* and they have *feelings*. They *remember* and make their *choices*. These are the attributes most basic to personhood. *Thinking* comprises of both reasoning and reflective understanding. *Feelings* cover a wide range of sensations that everyone is familiar with. *Memory* is a large and influential part of life, as is making *choices*. All this corresponds with what is known about God, who holds these modes in their perfection.

Biology and psychology are interested in how the many facets of awareness come about. For instance, the feeling of pain is directly related to the brain. For years my wife worked with intellectually disabled students and once taught a boy who never felt pain. Neither did he have any idea of pain in others, which led to challenging situations. With regard to memory though, does it belong to the brain exclusively or also the nervous system? The verdict isn't out on that one. And how do emotions happen? The sciences have found no definitive answers to that either, which is hardly surprising when in their experiments the reality of spirit is ignored. For instance, feelings of love are unlikely to be solely a material phenomenon, though affectivity may be restricted by brain malfunction.

The Bible does not address questions of where ability and the senses originate. It is not a scientific document, but a record of God and people – of Israel's history, the Gospel and the Early Church. Modes of awareness and where they might be placed within personhood, Scripture takes no interest in. They are accepted as occurring by God's design and all the Bible is concerned with is how to make the best of that, how to look after the soul in a way that fosters wellbeing.

When considering belonging, becoming, turning and relating, the four basic *demands* of the soul, it is *belonging* upon which the others develop. The pivotal point with the *modes* of soul awareness is the ability of *choice*. It is highlighted in the Genesis creation story which revolves around making choices; those by Adam and Eve, which alludes to the choices to be made by Jesus many years later. Genesis 2 depicts the human condition and gives insights on what life actually is about. Also today, choice remains central to how life will be lived, the quality of it. God knows that people tend to cope with life as best they can and, unless acts of evil become intentional, takes no issue with mistakes. Rather, God seeks to help with an enablement that is called grace.

This enablement comes into its own when following Jesus. Having been 'born again' though is no guarantee in itself of psycho-spiritual health. Such health requires a commitment to the fruit of the spirit. Psycho-spiritual wellbeing in Christ is readily available but depends on choices made. There is a journey to be walked — nothing heroic and simply good wisdom — that with the Lord's help will allow life to blossom. Jesus encourages towards it with a fine promise. 'Take my yoke upon you, and learn from me; for I am gentle and lowly at heart, and you will find rest for your souls' (Matt. 11:29). The *choice* is mine.

A great deal depends on a person's *disposition* of spirit, those fundamental desires and moods within the depths of awareness. With *belonging* being the premier 'demand' of the soul, for 'modes of awareness' *disposition* is most important – the nature of my *choices*. Wellbeing is much influenced by my sense of belonging and by disposition. It conditions my feeling and thinking. Scripture contains many an advice about life in this regard. In fact, the NT focuses as much on disposition as it does on the work of Christ. A need for the fruit of the spirit has already been mentioned. Then there is the great commandment to love God, yourself and people (Mark 12:29-31) and of course the golden rule not to do unto others what you won't like to happen to yourself. Disposition determines much.

9

Place-making

The importance of 'place' is underestimated and not an idea at the forefront of people's minds. Places come and places go. Moving from one place to another is common. Home is a place and hopefully a significant one. But few consider 'place' to be psychologically important. They simply never think about it

Scripture leaves no doubt about people being in need of a place. Adam and Eve became displaced when sent out of Eden. They lost their safe environment plus a place with God that was untroubled by sin. They became disenfranchised from divine reality and burdened under worldly pressures. Very much like people today.

Good places are essential for the wellbeing of soul but may not be that readily found. It needs someone to offer a significant place – of acceptance and association. Ideally, that happens while growing up in a family, when experiencing genuine care and belonging. In adulthood I can then offer a place to others, not just physically but in my heart. I can go anywhere and make there a place for myself, for I carry my original familial place within my soul, everywhere. I will know that I belong, even when miles away from significant others. Without such a sense of place however soul security is much diminished. It is a sad reality in life that the world is full of inferior places.

God is a place-maker. A place with God penetrates deeply within the spirit and is like no other in its potential. Psalm 118:5 reads (NKJV): 'I called on the Lord in distress; The Lord answered me and set me into a broad place.' The RSV translates the Hebrew texts as 'and set me free.' The idea here is one of salvation, of someone finding true liberty. The Psalm is one of victory and joy, of freedom for spirit and soul. Psalm 23 describes better than any other how beautiful a place with God can be. 'He leads me beside still waters, he restores my soul.' For good reason, it is the most loved Psalm.

Place-making is important and a firm disposition towards it is the key to success. I must w*ant* to discover my best place with God. I must *want* to be a good place-maker for others. I must be convinced how crucial it is to the wellbeing of myself and those in my care.

Place-making involves the four basic needs of soul awareness, needs that cannot be eradicated and must be attended to. A simple visualisation explains it, with the left side mentioning *belonging* and *becoming* being the more passive. They find their significance from being involved with other people who will embrace me. The right side of *turning* and *relating* is active – it shows what I must do, the choices to make.

$$\begin{array}{ccc} \textbf{Becoming} & \rightarrow & \textbf{Turning} \\ \uparrow & \textbf{1} & \downarrow \\ \textbf{Belonging} & \leftarrow & \textbf{Relating} \end{array}$$

Clockwise:
Belonging means finding a place of acceptance. Ideally unconditionally.
Becoming means that such a place helps me grow.
Turning asks that I respond positively towards where I belong and towards my development as a person.
Relating invites me to express that. And in doing so it nurtures my sense of *belonging*.

The figure '**1**' represents *wholeness*.

In a unified development of personhood every factor finds a meaningful expression. All works together as one. Though superficially matters may appear a little turbulent at times. Like teenage troubles in a good family, when growing into maturity is a challenging process.

I once discussed the place-making concept with someone in charge of a large team of people; how employees need a sense of being valued and taken seriously. How a feeling of *belonging* makes it easier for someone to accept the need of personal *growth* within the job. They will more readily *turn* towards the demands upon them and I feeling secure *relate* their ideas and difficulties with less hesitation. How, when responded to with care, it will strengthens *belonging*. In case difficulties arise, each aspect of the little model must be evaluated and the sticking points to be addressed with empathy. It will make for a healthy business culture. 'I can use this,' was the unhesitant response. 'It's simple and profound.'

The equation works anticlockwise equally. When I belong, I find it easier to relate. Good relating makes turning towards, rather than away, less problematic. I feel positive about it. Such turning helps me to grow which, increases understanding and makes me appreciate the value of real belonging more clearly. None of this is surprising. It easily rings true from experience and confirms the model's validity. Experiencing the basic demands of the soul is an integrated process and surely more complex than a simple formula can express. But it helps.

In soul awareness the most immediate sense of place is the space I feel to have when walking around within myself. Do I breathe easily? What is my inner place like? Is it the broad place the psalmist alluded to, or do I feel boxed in? I might know of spaces within myself I would rather not enter, or are unable to. Do I have a sense of God within my inner space or am I too timid, or fearful even, to dwell on this question? Perhaps I am satisfied with the state of my faith and leave God unknowingly at bay. 'Behold I stand at the door and knock,' the Lord says (Rev. 3:20). Open the door and I will come in and spend time with you. It often is taken as a call to salvation, but in Revelation it is a call to spiritual enlargement for people who were neither hot nor cold. It also applies when feeling reluctant before the Lord, for whatever reason. Jesus seeks to lead beside still waters, which presents an invitation towards creating much space within soul and overcoming the challenges of life.

The best place-makers are people who have found a congenial place within themselves. They understand what it takes to offer real places. Spiritually and relationally you can only give out what you have acquired. The best way in becoming well equipped is allowing the Lord to assist, leading into maturity. Place-making is a spiritual process.

The importance of the four basic demands of the soul in finding a place with God can be theologically explained as well. It reads as follows.

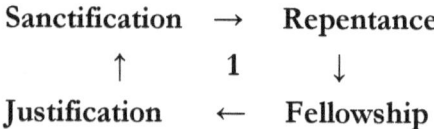

In Christ, God offers me a place of intimate *belonging*, I am *justified*. I have been accepted unconditionally into God's love and care. How much I will come to enjoy this special place is up to me and depends on choices made – on my disposition.

I must *become* more like Jesus, which is known as *sanctification*. With a heart towards God, the Lord will do a healing work within me over time. Thus I will find increasingly more space within my soul to walk around in for my place is broadening out. In God's enablement (grace) I find my liberation.

The benefits of justification and sanctification are what happens within me when open to their dynamics. Repentance and fellowship are different; I will have to make that happen.

The word *repentance* means a *turning* towards the better and positive. It may involve a highlight event when presented with a decision towards salvation, but generally concerns a persistent following in the ways of the Lord and turning away from the questionable. Life will tests this again and again and it remains a learning curve. Soul awareness needs to stay sharp and slip-ups will be frequent. God is merciful and patient.

Turning is a *relational* expression, which in a Christian context means *fellowship* with other believers and with God. Apostle Paul in his benediction at the end of the second letter to the Corinthians wishes the fellowship of the Holy Spirit to be with the church. A place with God becomes meaningful through relating. It presents as a choice to involve God in all of my life and not only the 'spiritual' side of it. It is by relating that my sense of identity strengthens and the nature of Christ within me develops. I often mentally relate to God and my sense of *belonging*, of having a place with God, thus is kept vibrant. It facilitates *becoming*, etc.

That leaves the meaning of the figure '1' to be explained theologically. It represents wholeness of being when each factor is properly active. The biblical concept of *shalom*, wellbeing for all, expresses it perfectly.

Walter Brueggemann notes an important aspect of *shalom* that, he says, is assumed rather than discussed in Scripture. 'It is the *shalom* sense of well-being, experienced by the *person* who lives a caring, sharing, joyous life in community' (1976, 20). Community inevitably involves problems and *shalom* in a congregational situation may be hard to find. In spite of this, at a person-to-person level much good can be achieved when relating well.

People, who sense a secure place within themselves, will be particularly effective in helping others find one also. Christians are encouraged to find such a place with God which, when properly understood, should translate into becoming a place-maker for others, especially so with immediate family and friends. From a good inner place, personally recognised and knowingly experienced, s*halom* can be offered to the world.

10

Soul Struggles

Oh my soul! My awareness of being is such a mixture of experiences. I am my body but more than my body. My spirit, I cannot grasp though it seems to be the enduring part of my being – eternally so, I am to believe. There is good in me, but bad lurks in the shadows. Oh my soul!, what have you got me into?

In Orthodox Russia there was a pilgrim in search of inner peace, which in spiritual theology is known as *hesychasm*. He could not find it until a Staretz (holy man) taught him to pray what is now called *The Jesus Prayer*. Over time this prayer began to repeat itself unaided within the soul of the pilgrim. 'But how wonderful, how delightful and how consoling a thing it is when God is pleased to grant the gift of self-acting spiritual prayer', the pilgrim exclaimed (French 1986, 15). He had found the way to pray without ceasing in his heart and the peace he was looking for. A focus on the prayer of the heart is central to Russian

Orthodox spirituality.

I introduced the prayer in one of my spirituality lectures. 'Jesus Christ, Son of God, have mercy on me, a sinner.' It has a beautiful rhythm and when repeated, mostly mentally, settles the spirit. One student took offence. 'I cannot pray that,' she said. 'I am no longer a sinner.' It is good theology – to a point. Apostle Paul clearly had his continuing struggles with the tempter. 'Who will deliver me?' he asked (Rom. 7:24). Jesus will, he declared and concluded: I am determined to serve the ways of God with my mind, but in my flesh (human nature) I am subject to the demands of sin.

I now sometimes replace the word sinner in the prayer with struggler. It surely sums up life nicely. In having discussed the nature of the soul thus far the word sin has only been mentioned superficially. There was no urgency for sin opposes the positive dynamics of the soul and adds nothing to its divine structure. But it does affect the quality of life negatively in a bad way. Everyone lives on struggle-street and as soul awareness that is acutely felt.

The biblical concept of sin became highlighted in the New Testament by the teachings of Paul, who offered the eternal liberation from sin to both Jew and Gentile. As an evangelist he faced a pagan culture that blurred the boundaries between good and evil in its practices. Consequently, the influences of sin in human behaviour, and the need for turning away from it, form a large part of Paul's letters to the churches. It remains essential advice today.

In the synoptic gospels (Matthew, Mark and Luke) the word sin doesn't much appear. The focus is on the walk of Jesus, his parables and the nature of his Father. It presents a God who cares, is close and is holy. The evil one was never ignored, but not given undue attention. It is a good rule for soul wellbeing. Focus on the positive while well aware of the negative pitfalls.

The gospel of John addresses the reality of sin more often, possibly because when written the Early Church was familiar with Paul's letters. John emphasised the spiritual nature of Jesus' mission and he recognised the significance of sin as the enemy accordingly.

The pitfalls of sin are inherent in human nature. The humanistic idea that all people are basically good is attractive, but mistaken. Not so the idea that people are able to develop their better nature and fortunately many seek to achieve just that. Jesus came to offer divine help in this struggle with the coming of the Holy Spirit. Available to all who are willing to seek such help.

The findings of modern psychology offers a large body of understanding that is worthwhile when in support of biblical instruction. The concepts of spirit and sin are foreign to psychology as active agents, but many of psychology's insights are relevant to wellbeing even so. Theories abound, for personhood is complex. Years ago, the book *Psychological Seduction* (1987) by William Kirk Kilpatrick was popular. It offered a veiled support of psychology, but suggested that its practices led away from God. In the sense that psychology helps a person to feel better and thus the need for God's grace is diminished.

This surely applies to Martin Seligman's ideas. The preface of his popular book *Authentic Happiness*, ends in stating that the road of Positive Psychology will lead you 'through the countryside of pleasure and gratification, up into the high country of strength and virtue, and finally to the peaks of lasting fulfilment: meaning and purpose' (2011, xiv). Seligman's beef is with the negativity imposed on society by the doctrine of original sin. His impressions of God, whose existence he now denies, clearly result from the 'sinners in the hands of an angry God' idea. The church must have never suggested otherwise to him; that God is love and care and immanently present. In *Meaning and Purpose*, the last chapter of his book, Seligman becomes philosophical with a teleological take on reality.

He ascribes to a win-win process in natural selection and disowns any idea of the divine reality as taught by Christianity.

> So there was no such God and there is no such God now. But, again, in the very longest run, where is the principle of win-win headed? Towards a God who is not supernatural, a God who ultimately acquires omnipotence, omniscience and goodness through the natural progress of win-win. Perhaps, just perhaps, God comes at the end (2011, 260).

'God' creates itself within creation over time. Build positively on personal strengths (forget weaknesses for they are negative) and existence can become pregnant with meaning, Seligman purports. Philosopher Scott Sehon sums it up nicely. 'When we think of human beings as physical objects, we use the language of physical science and we give causal accounts' (2005, 3).

Nevertheless, Seligman's book contains helpful information and his view on pessimism is not foreign to Christian believers. Church preaching may well focus overly much on human deficiencies instead of the liberating grace of Christ. Frequently, it warns rather than empowers, while it should do both. Seligman advises optimism, against a pessimism that he considers the result of society's history with Christianity. About psychology he suggests that it has focussed overly much on finding problems to address in people rather than taking a positive, confident approach that offers developmental opportunities. No wonder that Positive Psychology, in a world searching for happiness and identity, is popular as self-help information and with the wellness industry. It is seen as an effective approach towards positive change.

A positive approach gets the best out of Scripture as well. When accepting that God is really interested in my wellbeing, the struggles of life will lessen. While God's Word is an aide towards self-understanding.

> For the word of God is living and active, sharper than any two-edged sword, piercing to the division of soul and spirit, of joints and marrow, and discerning the thoughts and intentions of the heart (Hebrews 4:12).

Seemingly stern words; but there are two ways of looking at it. These verses are written in the context of finding rest in God; as a warning to not end up outside of that rest due to an unwise disposition. It may likewise be concluded from the text that God is aware of what I need to succeed in my life. A few verses on it mentions that in Jesus we have a high priest who knows how to sympathise with our weaknesses (Hebrews 4:15). I am invited to take on a positive disposition of secure dependence before a loving God, while I am doing my best.

The workings of sin belong to the very fabric of creation and inescapably need a response when manifesting in personhood with people able to distinguish between the good and the bad. As noted earlier, for all his trying, Apostle Paul could not live up to the life he wished for himself because of the negative influences imbedded into his being. He concluded that, 'I of myself serve the law of God with my mind, but with my flesh I serve the law of sin' (Rom. 7: 25). What must be noted is that success begins with the nature of one's mind, which Paul further addresses in Romans 8. Dealing with sin is hard work and requires remaining alert. Always sin will push the soul towards the unprofitable. Sin is deceptive and seek to convince of that which does harm. One of its lies suggests that dealing with God is difficult, which has excused many a person from trying to properly connect with God. Christians not excluded, who might prefer the mind of Self above the mind of Christ.

A.W. Tozer ends a chapter called *God is easy to live with* as follows:

> Some of us are religiously jumpy and self-conscious because we know that God sees our every thought and is acquainted with all our ways. We need not be. God is the sum of all patience and the essence of kindly good will. We please him most, not by frantically trying to make ourselves good, but by throwing ourselves into His arms with all our imperfections, and believing that He understands everything and loves us still (1991, 122).

God's Spirit has many ways in helping the soul to counter the negative influences of sin that are ingrained into earthly existence. A believer can assist them with prayer and bible-reading. Its effectiveness depends on how this reading is done and a superficial approach will not offer much benefit. While a reading that lacks a conviction of God's love and mercy might be discouraging; when personal shortcomings begin to hold centre stage. When 'Thou shalt not' is lurking in the mind as an accusation. The Ten Commandments were culturally important for the cohesion and wellbeing of Israel's society. At a personal level, they encouraged towards holiness. The seemingly stern words of 'Thou shalt not' are also a positive guide towards wellbeing and happiness.

All of God's directives are meant to do me well. I worship a God who is willing and imminently present. Bodily ailments, God will support me in those. Spiritual heaviness, Jesus is my burden sharer. My soul awareness may feed itself with good manna from Scripture. Helpful insights from sources such as psychology can also nourish my understanding. Living well is not easy and will have its struggles. The key to success is walking Struggle Street together with the Lord.

11

Grounding the Soul

Soul awareness is a vulnerable reality laden with anxieties and desires. In many ways soul remains a mystery. Every person copes with its dynamics as best they can. The challenges in managing what is happening to and in us are many. Always, we are drifting on a sea of change in which personality traits and relational imprints, healthy or not, determine much. The spaces in which I find myself, both externally and within my soul, condition many of my experiences. There is no single blueprint for success, as self-help books and its wide variety of topics confirm. This lucrative branch of the publishing industry shows how much people feel the need for improving their coping efficiencies. These books offer easy digestible solutions towards successfully managing anxieties and desires so that soul awareness becomes more focused and congenial. The surface waves of experience are being somewhat flattened. But deep seated vulnerabilities remain ever ready to bubble up disturbingly. Grounding the soul is a diverse process as would be clear by now and a brief reiteration of the information given thus far may be of help.

Life is complicated especially in how to stabilise the deeper self. It is effectively achieved by a modification of disposition. Harmful tendencies residing in the soul need adjusting towards more a wholesome approach. Creation has been designed so that wellness is best arrived at by principles that God has implanted within creation. Those principles are intrinsic to the nature of Presence and are ever active. Spirit/soul has access to these principles with their sense of validity being strengthen as psycho-spiritual health improves. Any person, regardless of belief, may benefit when aspiring to the God-given principles.

The nature of Presence is reflected in expressions of life that project love and care. Everyone faces this choice towards what is good – the choice of ego liberation through unselfishness against that of ego-centricity. A decent and caring life strengthens the power of universal love that resides in everyone's spirit and actualises the divine pattern towards wholeness inherent in Presence. About everyday living, Jesus declared that those who have done *good* will enjoy the resurrection of life rather than judgment (John 5:29). Doing good matters greatly, regardless of skin or creed.

A general adherence to Christianity can make life comfortable and secure. But a truly Christian lifestyle, one is which the soul will blossom well and bear fruit, is a different matter. It will require special effort. Like a house, identity is best built on a solid foundation in which knowing what you are aspiring to is paramount. Insight regarding this is helped by understanding God well.

When Jesus walked through Israel, he was aware how little his audiences knew about what his Father was really like and he challenged the self-perception of his hearers. Jesus highlighted the need for a change of heart, as many of the great prophets before him had. Many hearts remained hardened while others felt attracted, the more ordinary people in particular. Jesus' mission was one of miracles by which to gain attention and of addressing the deeper nature of people with teaching and parables. What exactly he was talking about remained, if not confusing, often difficult to achieve. But Jesus never shunned from the ideal for that would not reflect the nature of his Father, nor the possibilities of a life with God.

Matthew 24:32-45, and the whole of Matthew 25, is a warning against inclinations that ignore wise living. Such as the fig tree that bears no fruit while it should. Not being watchful in the knowledge that Christ can return at any time. Unfaithful service to a good master. The parable of the ten virgins. The parable of the talents. Opening yourself to judgment because of a wrong attitudes. Not to mention the washing of feet (John 13) and doubting Thomas (John 20). So much of what Jesus talked about, and did, concerned the proper grounding of the deep nature of the spirit/soul.

In doing 'good', the support that the soul gains from Presence may be compared to growing strawberries. A seedling is completely ignorant of whether it has been planted in average soil or better. It simply starts developing depending on the weather. Its little roots seek out where to find nourishment. Some roots may hit a small rock, while others find a bit of compost, which is what the roots are looking for. Enough compost with regular water will make beautiful strawberries kiss the sunshine. Not that the strawberries have any idea how this comes about as it does.

This story depicts a grounding of the soul. Soul has 'roots' that travel deep beyond the level of consciousness by means of spirit. Whether good nourishment will be found depends on the nature of a person's spirit. A spirit hardened towards what is good will find the soil barren and bear little fruit. While a spirit seeking God's ways may draw from moist, well composted, ground. These positive dynamics of growth supported by spirit are real and happening though soul awareness will not know of it but by faith. Over time the benefits will show, when faith is rewarded, and life will feel to be better grounded.

In growing towards producing fruit the strawberry roots will have to displace some soil. There is a resistance to overcome. Likewise, the progress of spirit/soul will confront opposition. Strength of purpose is needed and a development of character to ensure success.

The need for character has not escaped modern-day thinkers – nor society. David Brooks' book *The Road to Character* (2015) became a bestseller. Martin Seligman addresses the importance of character in a section of his popular book *Authentic Happiness* (2002). Character is what it takes to be your own person, he concludes. It is what people are looking for.

Apostle Paul went as far as to say that he rejoiced in the difficulties being faced in proclaiming the Gospel of Christ. He would not let suffering discourage him. The good thing is, he suggested, that it built character. It strengthened his hope and conviction that God's enablement dwelled within him through the Holy Spirit (Rom. 5:1-5). There is no gain without some pain, at least not in matters of value. Character is like a shock absorber. It stabilises you on the road of life.

Character aids towards a well-grounded soul. For it to be effective though it needs a frame of reference, something to believe in about yourself. That realisation was what kept Apostle Paul going. The influences of sin will always be troubling, as Paul was sorely troubled. He responded by keeping the ways of God firmly at the front of his mind (Rom. 7: 7-25). In this, there is no need for perfection, merely that of having the right intention with some solid trying. In it all, God's spirit is a helper, always.

It is true that a large part of God's being will forever be hidden. That has translated into the idea of God as 'Wholly Other'; a faraway divine reality best engaged with through spiritual exercises. There is some validity in that approach. My studies of spiritual theology have made me familiar with those exercises and I enjoy contemplation. Progressively however I came to see that when mystical experience senses a transcendental reality it is no more, or less, than a particular experience of God in which divine reality becomes a little more revealed. But from a divine perspective, will it really bring someone nearer to God? I wouldn't think so, for with all of creation existing *in* God, who is aware of the number of hairs on my head (not too many in my case), how much closer can you get? God's counting of hairs is not a divine intellectual exercise over a distance, but rather a complete knowing relationally, in love. Sin is no obstruction to this for it cannot hinder God's love, and neither is unbelief. Any apparent obstruction is my doing.

It is never a question of whether God is present, but how soul awareness perceives this. Some experience the divine presence through visions (the mystics), others by faith (the Christian) and many not much, if at all (the non-believer). Yet always, God is near.

It is difficult to get a correct sense of God unless desiring to live in accordance with the nature of Christ. Failing to do this characterises the false mystic and lukewarm Christian, when an ego-centric approach dulls the spirit and fills the soul with unhealthy vibrations. If I have not love, I'm but a clanging cymbal, Paul declared (1Cor. 13:1).

With the right approach to my Christian life I may by faith assume an intimacy with God which need not be dependent on emotions. Feeling flat or agitated makes no difference to the reality of the Lord being close. Nor does heightened emotions mean that God is any closer. Not to say that having a real sense of God's presence isn't a worthwhile and wonderful experience to seek after. Still, whatever a day may bring, I can remain confident in being okay and grateful that the Holy Spirit is my helper. Thus my soul will remain well grounded.

12

A Deep Nature

Soul awareness and the idea of mind are closely related. When people talk about the mind it is readily understood what is being referred to. But what exactly mind is, nobody is sure about. Every language would have a terminology regarding mental activity. The English Bible uses the word mind about 200 times in translating from the original text of Scripture. Often not quite accurately, for the original has shades of meaning that are non-translatable. English itself speaks of mind in so many different ways that a concise definition is not possible. Any explanation will be lengthy and at best descriptive.

Perhaps you find this *mind*-boggling. Or not, and you prefer for me to *mind* my own business. For you are quite able to make up your own *mind* about the matter. After all, great *minds* need not always think alike. I'd do best to be *mind*-full of it and my practice of *mindfulness* may help. Ah well, never you *mind*. As long as we both have the *mind* of Christ. No need to be *doubleminded* about it.

Personhood much depends on the idea of having a mind. Throughout history it has been reflected on. In modern days the mind and brain are considered inseparable with the mind/brain mystery at the forefront of modern physiological studies. Pioneers in neurobiology suggest that mind is simply a brain phenomenon. Others are not so sure and opinions differ. A Christian point of view holds that the reality of spirit must be acknowledged when seeking to understand the origin and functioning of the mind. Also then, definitive insights will remain elusive.

Mind and brain function are intricately related. Malfunction of the brain affects the mind, raising the question whether when consciousness is lost, the mind no longer functions. Thomas Aquinas, like many others, held that mind extends beyond consciousness, a perspective which I consider correct. René Descartes believed that consciousness is able exist in isolation of the body, as did American philosopher/psychologist William James. It implies that the mind, when seen as vital to consciousness, might function as a 'spirit' phenomenon. Whereby, Wittgenstein suggested that there may be mental activities that lack any correlate in the brain. 'Why should there not be a psychological regularity to which *no* physiological regularity corresponds? If this upsets our concept of causality, then it is high time it was upset' (Kenny 2010, 921). Ideas about 'mind' are many.

Much of the deeper workings between brain and mind remain hidden to awareness. It reminds of entering a busy railway terminal. Some of the major stations around the world are vast and have a fine architecture with massive domes and are beautifully built. Trains coming and going and people everywhere. All sorts is happening. From purchasing a ticket to having a coffee or meal; with the option of lockers for luggage and an information kiosk to possibly book further travel or a hotel. Not to mention all the work of the personnel that keep this show on the rails. So many people and so much noise. When I look around, I can see a little of it all at best. However, that little is sufficient to make me aware of being in a significant station. It is what my railway experience is like. Quite substantial, particularly when I plan to travel, but very limited in what city central rail altogether is about.

My experience of mind/brain is similar. Soul awareness, the conscious side of living, is only a small aspect of what is happening within me in response to incessant sensory input. Tor Norretranders wrote a fascinating book about it called *The User Illusion*. He quotes from a lecture in 1965 by German physiologist Dietrich Trincker.

> Of all the information that every second flows into our brains from our sensory organs, only a fraction arrives in our consciousness: the *ratio* of the capacity of *perception* to the capacity of *apperception* is at best a million to one. …. That is to say, only *one millionth* of what our eyes see, our ears hear, and other senses inform us about *appears in our consciousness* (1991, 126).

How the brain discards so much input and makes me aware of only little is a mystery. But it does. The mind, when taken as the immaterial side of brain function, is deeper than the soul, for soul is solely an awareness. Mind involves both body and spirit. As such it may be suggested that it plays a part in dealing with the myriad of sensory inputs that the body is confronted with and the brain makes conscious, or does not. There is much happening beyond sentience as well. Human capacity in dealing with data is enormous, with memory, will, inspiration, wisdom, disposition, language, thinking, choice, and emotions thought to be partly stored inside the nervous system. Whatever the accuracy of this, the subconscious is vast. I know myself only in part and no better than what the soul reveals and I am aware of. About this awareness Norretranders writes:

> Consciousness is ingenious because it knows what is important. But the sorting and interpretation required for it to know what is important is *not* conscious. Subliminal perception and sorting is the real secret behind consciousness (1991, 174).

The mind takes information from body, spirit and soul. It responds to body sensations, spirit input and interprets soul awareness. As such it may be said that a person's identity is determined by the mind. 'As in water face answers to face, so the mind of man reflects the man' (Prov. 29:19). Elsewhere in Proverbs it explains that the spirit side of a person illuminates everything about her before the Lord, who thus is able to search that person's innermost parts (Prov. 20:27). It suggests that spirit-wise a person is extended beyond what may be called 'mind'. After all, spirit accesses the very depth of Presence where the total person finds its life and possibilities. The idea of 'mind' will remain flexible, as the demarcations between body, soul and spirit will be.

The human experience of mind is cognitive. People realise they are of a certain mind even though they may give it little thought. The idea of mind covers a wide spectrum. The modern trend towards mindfulness has characteristics that belong more to spirit. When insisting that the mind has an exclusively material origin, as Steve Pinker does in his book *How the Mind Works*, questions present that remain unresolved. Such as the fact that brain studies offer no answer to where sentience comes from.

> As far as scientific explanation goes, it might as well not exist. It's not just that claims about sentience are perversely unstable; it's that testing them would make no difference to anything anyway. Our incomprehension of sentience does not impede our understanding of how the mind works in the least (Pinker 1997, 147).

This only makes sense, if by mind Pinker means brain function, which he does. What occurs beyond that function, though possibly related to it, is of no scientific interest. Pinker's is a narrow and insufficient use of the concept of mind.

That consciousness, and thus both soul and mind, are

dependent on brain function is without question. Apply chemicals to the brain and a total loss of awareness may occur, e.g. with a general anaesthetic, while a local anaesthetic blocks the pain signals and results in a partial loss of sensation. Drugs of all kinds affect the brain. They can diminish stimuli, as anti-depressants do, or stimulate beyond the ordinary into hallucinations. The boundaries of normal brain function can be crossed in many ways. Ecstasy induced through religion practices does just that. Always there are dangers when reaching beyond the ordinary and the psyche can become unhinged. While personality changes are not uncommon when the brain has been damaged thus permanently modifying soul awareness.

That the idea of 'mind' is a divine one Apostle Paul shows when writing about the mind of the Spirit.

> Likewise the Spirit helps us in our weakness; for we do not know how to pray as we ought, but the Spirit himself intercedes for us with sighs too deep for words. And he who searches the hearts of men knows what is the mind of the Spirit because the Spirit intercedes for the saints according to the will of God. We know that in everything God works for good with those who love him. (Rom. 8:26-28).

The Spirit has in mind what God has in mind for the wellbeing of the believer and intercedes accordingly. In another of his letters, Paul encourages us to pray with confidence and thanksgiving, 'and the peace of God, which passes all understanding, will keep your hearts and your minds in Christ Jesus' (Phil. 4:7). The word heart here refers to disposition and that of mind to one's mental state. Best to 'gird up your minds,' Apostle Peter suggests (1Peter 1:13). The new spirit within the Christian can be activated by faith and determination, which helps in overcoming the ways of the world.

Mind, in common understanding, is a flexible concept. No two minds are quite the same and often will be very different. But everyone has a mind that manifests in soul awareness. The nature of mind is deeper than that of soul. It is facilitated by the brain and resides in spirit. Unlike the soul that disappears at death, the mind remains. It is what God will evaluate at the Pearly Gates. Mind is of a deep nature that rises up into human awareness as soul. An awareness that is able to discern and follow the mind of Christ. People are wonderfully made.

13

The Thinking Soul

I have been thinking about how to begin this chapter. My mind going through the various things I would like to say. An exercise of sorting through facts. But also I just sat reflectively for a while waiting for a possible idea that would make for a good introduction. There were no facts or mental words involved in this process, but a kind of expectancy for something worthwhile to come to mind out of the quiet. Some would say that proper thinking is actually about that. Engaging in possibilities that are waiting to be discovered. Many of the great ideas have arrived in this way, like Einstein's fourth dimension. The special Eureka moment. Commonly though, thinking is considered to be a logical or evaluative progression sifting through data.

Everyone has thoughts and it is taken for granted. But at second thought, this mental ability is nothing short of amazing. What makes it even possible that people can think? Because of an organ of jelly-like grey matter within a skull? It beggars belief. Not that there would be insufficient cells and neuro transmitters in the brain to manage the process. Obviously, there are. But how can material processes result into non-material, cognitive understandings that are creatively operative? Something related, but other than the brain, must be involved.

When Descartes concluded, 'I think, therefore I am,' he was right enough. Particularly, when it is understood that his use of the word 'think' has a broader meaning than generally understood. 'As always in Descartes "thought" is to be understood broadly: thinking is not always to think *that* something or other, and not only intellectual meditation but also volition, sensation and emotion count as thoughts' (Kenny 2010, 660). Much of what involves consciousness falls under the category of thinking, according to Descartes. Perhaps his famous statement might also read: 'I am aware, therefore I am.'

Descartes use of 'think' is unusual and shows how the word has been applied in an expanded fashion. Historically, the idea of thinking is associated with the human ability to 'reason'; already in the days of Socrates, Plato and Aristotle – and earlier times. Competent reasoning was considered the queen of accomplishments. Everyone can agree that good thinking offers a distinct handle on life. Life becomes more manageable that way, whether philosophically or practically. Modern society is mostly a fruit of thought. It stores up its knowledge and develops incredible technologies. Intellectual achievements never stop progressing.

Thinking is an interpretive response to reality. It is a focussed process that looks for insights and solutions based on how life is experienced. The power of thought is broad ranging whereby stimuli can be circumstantial or may arise from within a person; situations that ask for a response, or an idea that needs attending to. Occasions for thought are manifold but for thoughts to qualify as thinking they must be intentional. Thoughts swirling through the mind willy-nilly are the flotsam of mental life and are not considered thinking proper.

Personhood is complex and the capacity of reason its puppet master. It directs the dance of life, or so it seems. Blaise Pascal (1623-1662) though pointed out years ago that, 'The heart has its reasons which reason knows not of' (1991, 230). Furthermore, the notion that intelligent people naturally will deal with life more rationally than those less so endowed is plainly wrong. David Robson in the introduction to *The Intelligence Trap* writes that, 'This book is why intelligent people act stupidly – and why in some cases they are even more prone to error than the average person' (2019, 2). Some of the examples he gives are astounding. Thinking has power, but it inevitable remains subjective. Brooks continues by suggesting that his book will help people 'to think more wisely and rationally in this post-truth world' (ibid.).

Philosopher Harry F. Frankfurt wrote a little book entitled *On Bullshit* which has found popularity in the Trump era. He distinguishes between the honest person and the liar, both of whom speak in reference to truth, and the bullshitter, who has no such qualms.

> ... he is neither on the side of the true nor on the side of the false. His eye is not on the facts at all .... except in so far as they may be pertinent to his interest in getting away with what he says (2005, 56).

Frankfurt explains that such people may come to believe in what they are saying as actually being true. That may well involve a lie that no longer is a lie to them.

Responsible thinking needs a frame of reference and cannot happen in a vague sort of way. It is careful and dependent on reliable data for good outcomes. The more grounded the data, the more readily can a worthwhile construct of thought be built. When thinking about life, and how to go about it, modern society has created a cauldron of swirling ideas in which little is found to be of lasting value. It is the post-truth world Brooks is referring to with life being transient and often superficial. Thinking is often done on the run and subject to unduly personal preferences, frequently to the point of intolerance. Its most serious manifestation is indoctrination – the lack of freedom of thought insisted on by those who feel free to impose the value of their own thoughts upon others. A value that may well be questionable.

A frame of reference for thinking that can be considered reliable will show dependable evidence of what it can achieve. Like, mathematics is attractive because it has a track record of results and thus can be safely committed to. Far more complex is committing to ideas about how to live a meaningful life. That search becomes an identity question of what essentially I am about. Elton Trueblood makes a pivotal observation:

> 'My own life cannot be unified except by that to which I am devoted. But where shall I turn? A mere "ism" will never suffice. Because persons are superior, in kind, not only to all *things* but even to all

ideas, I need a person to whom I can give myself and thereby find myself. But not just any person will suffice; it must be a person commitment to whom can change the imperfect world order.' (1979, 45).

Trueblood is concerned about the unification of life. Not life that switches from this to that in what is thought to be important, but life that has found a firm foundation of understanding on which to base effective thinking. Ideas of significant others, particularly those with a proven track record, will be helpful in this. Libraries are full of books that are good source material. Trueblood though raises the bar by insisting that 'isms' are insufficient when seeking a framework of ideas that can change the world for the better. Ideas alone then will not suffice. Mere theory won't do. It needs a special person to whom to safely commit, someone with ideas the fruits of which are clearly apparent from life well lived. The ultimate person will be Christ, of course. He who came 'not as a Seeker, but rather as a Revealer who tells us what He knows, not what he has deduced' (Trueblood 1979, 43).

Thinking is a powerful dynamic in soul awareness. It dictates and can alter life for better or worse; a fact well recognised in Scripture.

> Whatever is true, whatever is honourable, whatever is just, whatever is pure, whatever is lovely, whatever is gracious, if there is any excellence, if there is anything worthy of praise, *think* about these things. What you have learned and received and heard and seen in me, *do*; and the God of peace will be with you (Phil. 4:8-9).

Apostle Paul was not shy in insisting that believers focus their thoughts profitably and in their actions follow his example. That approach to life is a sure way into the presence of God. 'Renew the spirit of your minds,' he exhorted, 'and put on the new nature created after the likeness of God' (Eph. 4:23-24).

I have found value from the Trinitarian Relational Model presented in my book *The Primacy of Love* (2015) as a theology and in *Living Well* (2021), as non-religious, self-help information suitable for everyone, in the realisation that God's principles apply across humanity and will bring well-being to all. The model recognises how the relational is basic to existence and is an expression of God's love. So is the opposite of love, the dynamic of sin, relational. The model offers practical insights on how to live well by knowing what works for good and what must be avoided. It involves a generic frame of reference about desired attitude and behaviour that derives from a study of the Trinity. I helps me sort out my thinking.

Thinking has a significant influence on how everyday life is experienced. In 1952 Norman Vincent Peale published *The Power of Positive Thinking* which, to everyone's surprise, became an absolute success that broke the all-time record for the length it remained on *The New York Times* bestsellers list. A new publishing genre resulted, the self-help genre that mostly focuses on mental adaptation. For people realise that changing your mind is possible with renewed thinking a skill to be learned. Preferably quickly and with immediate success. All kinds of personal growth possibilities are addressed, including desires. *Think and Grow Rich* (1937), by Napoleon Hill, is but one example that has lasted the distance. Thought modification is central to Cognitive Therapy, a psychological discipline that encourages positive mind control.

The benefits of a positive approach in coping with life has become quite popular in psychology. Martin Seligman published a book called *Learned Optimism* (1991). He is best known these days for *Authentic Happiness* (2002), mentioned earlier, in which he sets out how to concentrate on your strengths and forget weaknesses.

The subtitle of the book reads: *Using the New Positive Psychology to Realise Your Potential for lasting Fulfilment.*

The main focus is on the question, 'what is there in it for me?' How can I improve my self-experience by directing my thinking towards the positive and thus achieve pleasure and gratification. It will need work and persistence, Seligman admits. He suggests to offer an outlook on life that will enhance authenticity. Many psychological studies confirm the idea of 'think well, that you may live well'. Apostle Paul understood it perfectly, though his advice was far less ego-centric. He pointed towards the One to commit to for a success that taps into the nature of God. The Person behind the best ideas.

Theology has always appreciated the power of thought. Much of theology prefers thought above a more esoteric approach to understanding God, such as intuition, which concerns spiritual theology and includes the experiencing of God and related insights. This branch of theology is considered to lack rigidity. Ever since the medieval Church with its prescriptive dominance, followed by the Enlightenment, spiritual theology has been seen as not theology proper. Though it must be noted that during medieval times a deep search for spiritual authenticity did occur as a response to ridged dogma and Church ritual.

The intuitive side of Christian religion has always been present, but never was popular with the establishment. These days that perspective is changing for the better, but slowly. Talking about God is much easier than talking as a friend of God.

The intellect has much to offer and theology has not run shy of seeking to explain the structure of consciousness. Bernard Lonergan's *Method in Theology* (1972) is an example. It suggests a sequence of cognitive steps by which a person internalises reality. Lonergan presents a transcendental method, 'that is concerned with meeting the exigences and exploiting the opportunities presented by the human mind itself (1972, 14). In other words, the methods concerns moments of experience and they are mentally interpretable in accordance with how the human mind is structured. Human ability is able to question awareness. People are using four levels of interpretation in dealing with what confronts them, says Lonergan, and do so by nature.

> Level 1 is *experiencing* – I become aware of something.
> Level 2 is *understanding* – I make sense of it.
> Level 3 is *judging* – I evaluate the sensation.
> Level 4 is *deciding* – I make up my mind how to

respond to the sensation.

This deciding is a fresh experience and the sequence of four steps begins all over again. Lonergan suggests that the mind continually works through the four levels and thus people make sense, properly or not, of whatever comes their way. It is how consciousness works.

At level 4, the one of deciding, morality (choice) applies. With morality being *a priori*, Lonergan suggests that this level offers possibilities of self-transcendence. The foundation of morality is love, a quality that reaches beyond the limitations of natural existence. Ideally, that love leads to Christ.

Lonergan's work is extensive. This brief introduction aims to give an idea how an intellectual approach to the nature of soul awareness allows for interesting insights.

The Neoplatonic tradition of Thomas Aquinas lives on. Thinking remains the dominant way in which to make sense of our universe with the sciences being a prime example. It is the logical way central to all academic disciplines. But there is more to soul awareness than the intellect alone.

14

The Feeling Soul

If thinking is the interpretative response to reality, feeling is the emotive one. The sensing of reality comes before its understanding. Thus personhood is felt first and then cognitively experienced. I sense that I am and interpret that mentally. The feeling side of this experience can be addressed in a number of ways, each coming well short of being comprehensive. Feelings essentially are not a mental phenomenon, as is clearly understood when deeply hurt by others or circumstances. When the body may curl itself around the stomach in a ball. Biblically, the pit of the stomach is considered to be the centre of where emotions resides.

Feeling responses can be psychosomatic where body affects spirit and vice versa. It is thought that 80% of bodily ailments originate from a troubled spirit/body interaction be that anxiety, depression, loneliness and so much more. While a happy disposition increases physical wellbeing. 'A cheerful heart is good medicine, but a downcast spirit dries up the bones' (Prov. 17:22.). Bill Bryson, in his book *The Body*, mentions how frequent positive relational activity lengthens the telomeres in one's DNA resulting in potential long-levity. 'It is an extraordinary fact that having good and loving relationships physically alters your DNA. Conversely, a 2010 US study found, not having such a relationship doubles your risk of dying from any cause' (2020, 437). These findings confirm scientifically how feelings affect bodily function.

Some years ago I was tired and jittery for long enough to seek out my doctor. I was found to be suffering from an overactive thyroid. The specialist asked whether I had been under a period of stress. I shook my shoulders wondering; not that I knew. She treated the condition with a course of tablets and 18 months on all was well. I felt no longer tired and strong in the knees, which fortunately has stayed that way. Quite some time later it dawned on me that actually there had been a particular stressful period in my life. Not that I ever considered it in that way always seeking to find some rest in Jesus whatever the circumstances. Obviously, I had not achieved it and fooled myself. Not a problem that, but I will avoid falling into that trap again and be extra wary about letting things bother me overly much. One can but try. Undoubtedly, my feeling unwell had a psychosomatic origin.

Feelings are inescapable and will present as they see fit. Some are simply to be lived through, while others are open to modification. 'Anxiety in a man's heart weighs him down, but a good word makes him glad' (Prov. 12:15). A friend can talk you out of the doldrums into feeling better as you begin to change your thinking. This has been studied in psychology and is the premise of Cognitive Behaviour Therapy (CT) and Rational Emotive Behavioural Therapy (REBT) both introduced by Albert Ellis and Robert A Harper. Their book *A Guide to Rational Living* (1961) has now sold over 1.5 million copies. It remains the got-to text for many in the people helping profession as well as the common reader. Although a correct cognitive response can change your outlook on life, Ellis and Harper admit that not *all* negative emotions can thus be eliminated – like grief or fear. They write:

> We flexibly contend: You can change your thinking and the emotions that go with it by discovering and changing your strong Beliefs. We hold, more importantly, that you often needlessly create unhealthy emotions – such as depression, anxiety,

> rage, and feelings of worthlessness – and that you can remodel them if you will change your thinking and follow it up with effective action (1997, 32).

Strong beliefs, when associated with negative feelings, are always wrong beliefs and unnecessary, it is suggested.

There is much in psychology along these lines, all based on empirical data. David D Burns book *Feeling Good: The New Mood Therapy* has sold over 3 million copies. It surprised Burns, who gives as reasons that the book's ideas are down-to-earth and intuitive while supported by many research studies as effective. Also, cognitive therapy has become hugely popular (1999, xvii). Burn's premise is that, 'The bad feelings we have in depression all stem from negative thoughts, therefore treatment must be about challenging and changing those thoughts' (Butler Bowdon 2007, 60). Self-blame often is a problem. 'Depressed people feel wretched even when they are loved, have a family, have good jobs, and so on. We can have "everything" but if self-love and self-worth have fled, we feel we are nothing,' Burns concludes (Butler Bowdon 2007, 60).

Another popular book is Robert E Thayer's *The Origin of*

Everyday Moods in which he recognises four basic moods. *Calm-energy* (high energy, low tension); *Calm-tiredness* (low energy, low tension); *Tense-energy* (high energy, high tension) and *tense-tiredness* (when you feel all used up). 'If we are in a dark mood, none of our achievements or our wealth matter to us; in a positive mood, even the worst circumstances seem manageable,' writes Thayer (Butler-Bowdon 2007, 286).

Feelings are deep waters and people react to it differently. Personality type partly determine responses to reality and its perceived threats. The 16 types of Myer Briggs based on introvert/extrovert, judging/perceiving, thinking/feeling and sensing/intuition are well known.

As are the Enneagram's 9 types based on how Sufi Masters sought to understand and guide their pupils. It has been popularised, for one, by priest Richard Rohr's *Discovering the Enneagram* (1990), a very accessible and helpful text for better self-understanding. Not only does it explain what a particular type is like; it points out strengths and weaknesses and the way forward towards better psychological health. In recognition that preferred modes of coping limit personal development as they become ingrained, Rohr explains that, 'The Enneagram shows us our compulsive styles of attention, which prevent us from experiencing reality holistically and honestly' (1991, 19). The book is Christ centred, though the Enneagram originates from Sufi wisdom.

When years ago I presented this wisdom to a group of young people, a girl told me it was great for now she understood who she was and felt more comfortable in her skin. She also better understood why others might seem to wonder about her interactions and would keep that insight in mind: that people approached life differently and might misjudge her. How rightly she spoke. It is of benefit to know how you tick deep within, the emotions and responses common to your personality. With the Enneagram as a guide, feelings can be better interpreted and responded to. It helps the soul in finding its comfort and the best way forward.

Psychology's answer to the phenomenon of feelings broadly speaking is fourfold. The analytic approach seeks to understand the origin of feelings (e.g. Sigmund Freud), while a developmental one focuses on stages of self-realisation (e.g. Maslow/Erickson). The humanistic approach encourages the expression of emotions in a group environment thus feeling liberated and presumably also better understood (e.g. Carl Rogers). While the behavioural/cognitive approach suggests to counteract feelings with a wilful modification of thought processes (see above).

That people flock to these insights taking therapy sessions and/or consulting books, shows how great the need is for an improved coping with self and with life; a problem that will never be lastingly solved. Psychology's research into the human condition must be lauded. People do function in ways that are open to study, and all by God's design.

Feelings arrive because of circumstances, your level of wellbeing, or of their own accord. The latter involve the deeper side of soul awareness and the spirit. Such feelings may drift up into awareness for whatever reason and reveal my innermost being more than my thoughts ever will. Potentially those feelings derive from the depth at which spirit interacts with the origin of my being – with Presence. Not that I would ever know about those dynamics where universal love and sin are in play. Perhaps it will translate into feelings of benevolence or temptation and most negatively into hatred. One can but surmise. It may involve the happenings of past living that are stored in my spirit beyond my reach, not as dead letters on a page but as active memories that possibly are dormant.

A well-known, distinctly spiritual experience, that can arise into awareness as a feeling without notice, is the dark night of the soul, explained by St John of the Cross (1542-1591). It involves a purification of a person's spirit to better align it with the ways of the Lord. Regarding this process, St John mentions two nights. The first, he calls the 'unspiritual night' that may be experienced by many a sincere Christian. The second one is the 'spiritual night', which reaches deeper into the psyche and is so taxing that only few will ever be invited into it. A dark night of the soul is initiated by God, will come as a surprise, and varies in length possibly lasting for a number of weeks. During this time God is felt as being distant and far away, which is an illusion. St John writes:

> There is another thing which causes the soul great distress at this time and which arises because the dark night has clouded the faculties and desires of the soul. This is that the soul cannot lift its mind or emotions, or even pray to God (1988, 64).

All this to quieten the innermost being of a believer so that God can do a psycho-spiritual healing work, the nature of which will remain hidden. Once the night has passed, the soul feels much the better for it senses an improved equilibrium and freedom. This must be cultivated and maintained through Christlike living.

A dark night touches those parts of me only known to God in which the Spirit will do its influential work. It is a special event at a particular time. That God is well able to offer general wellbeing at *all* times is clear from what Jesus said.

> Come to me all who labour and are heavy laden, and I will give you rest. Take my yoke upon you, and learn from me; for I am gentle and lowly in heart, and you will find rest for your souls. For my yoke is easy, and my burden is light (Matt. 11:28-30).

What stands out in this invitation is the Lord's gentleness and being lowly in heart. Not at all like the pressures put upon people by worldly affairs. Jesus knows what being human, and its challenges, is like first-hand. He promises living water to flow out of my innermost being (John 7:38). Abundant life is on offer (John 10:10). These are qualities of spirit for a Christian to enjoy, as is the Lord's offer of grace enablement. A new kind of living may be experienced by those who reach out for it with sincerity and confidence.

Soul awareness will find its most beneficial responses

to the emotive side of personhood when taking advice from Jesus. Difficult suggestions like to forgive or, as Paul suggests, not to let the sun go down upon anger, begin to make good sense for it settles emotions. The wisdom needed in managing life well will be supported by that still small voice. Unsurprisingly, none of this is automatic. Jesus invites us to learn from him and be taught gently without reproof so that the soul to be equipped and strengthened while facing the challenges of daily life

Emotions are deep waters from which all kinds of sensations continually rise up. Happy experiences are great, but not so those that contain heaviness and frustration. Sometimes this negativity may be short circuited by an activity like going for a walk. Perhaps a good night's sleep is needed. When sorely troubled I tend to slide into my bed early and usually soon fall asleep due to weariness. The next morning things are looking different, not as bad. A popular way in countering troublesome feelings is the intake of substances such as alcohol, which is not necessarily wrong when done in moderation. Substance abuse however always lurks around the corner. Drugs are problematic and how often do we not read about famous people who are under pressure committing suicide. Managing feelings can be a slippery slope.

Christians don't escape from it either for there is no magic wand. The best way to cope with our inner vulnerabilities is staying close to the Lord without whitewashing problems, which are well known to God anyway. In getting a handle on things I tend to take a three step approach – the three Cs. Firstly, I tell myself to take a deep breath and *calm* down. 'Lord help me with your peace.' There is no need to be all in a muddle. Secondly, I decide to take *control* and insist to myself that in Christ I am able to manage what I am faced with. 'I can do all things in him who strengthens me' (Phil. 4:13). And thirdly, I will put on *confidence* with a courage that will help me succeed. In Philippians 4, the word 'rejoice' in NT Greek contains the idea of being 'quietly confident'.

> Rejoice I the Lord always; again I say rejoice. Let all men know your forbearance. The Lord is at hand. Have no anxiety about anything, but in everything by prayer and supplication with thanksgiving let your request be made known to God. And the peace of God, which passes all understanding, will keep your hearts and your minds in Christ Jesus (Phil. 4:4-7).

Feelings are a powerful dynamic in soul awareness that is ever active. There is nothing a person does in which feelings will not play a part. I constantly acknowledge them before the Lord, whether good or bad, and where appropriate make them subject by thinking right to the overriding principles I seek to live by. I also realise that feelings can be irrational or unhelpful and then use my mind to set that straight. It will be demanding at times, with failure not uncommon, but surely is the best way. Whatever the complication, a life without feelings is a song without a voice.

15

The Spirited Soul

Thinking and feeling sensations are immediate and inescapable. Less so the spirited influences that affect consciousness. What originates from the spirit side of being often remains undetected. It operates subliminally and can be quite powerful. Understanding soul/spirit expressions belongs to psychoanalysis and spiritual discernment in particular. These are considerable fields of knowledge acquired through study. Not something most people are familiar with. So how best to get some insights regarding the spirited soul for everyday use?

The Christian has an advantage in that Scripture reveals a lot about personhood and the influences of God on the human spirit. All the same, those influences usually remain subtle and acknowledgement of their happening rests on faith. Faith in that what God's Spirit promises, it will achieve, quite apart from my feeling that way. Over time God will guide and enable through spirit influences towards becoming a person with a secure identity of self. 'To thine own self be true,' is a much uttered exclamation, which is unavoidably correct. No-one can be true to the self of someone else, though that is not what the phrase is referring to, of course. It encourages to stick by your convictions and know what those are. That becomes problematic when the self is rather superficial, not solidly grounded within; when little is residing in the self that elicits loyalty. The post-modern identity is predominantly social, in which the self finds meaning in interacting with others. Stanley Grenz observed that this self 'is highly decentered and fluid, as a person can have as many selves as social groups in which he or she participates' (2001, 76). So what about the self? Is it merely a matter of projected identity or does the reality of self originate from far deeper in the human psyche?

Søren Kierkegaard (1813-1855) held that the awareness of self is the criterion of self. You cannot knowingly be what you do not detect about yourself. Furthermore, you can never become your ultimate self, Kierkegaard insisted, unless you accept that the potential originates with God and needs to be developed. 'The more conception of God, the more self; the more self, the more conception of God. Only when the self as this definite individual is conscious of existing before God, only then is it the infinite self,' Kierkegaard wrote (Benner 1998, 79). To know who you are, and that before God, makes possible the ultimate fulfilment of what self is meant to be. Like Kierkegaard, ancient Hebrew understanding held that the knowledge of God and that of self are reciprocal. Improved self-understanding increased the understanding of God and vice versa. In which biblical morality is the standard whereby to evaluate this understanding.

The infinite self, mentioned by Kierkegaard, is being realised when a person lives in relationship with God, as like a child of a heavenly Father. That self, now having improved access to its perfect Form in Presence, is able to become fully actualised. Every self is eternal and while on earth is invited to grow in accordance with the divine nature. In my view, a healthy realisation of self surely is possible for those who seek to follow 'the good' even though not acknowledging Christ. The Spirit of God is ever active and particularly a helper to those who reflect the divine nature in their intentions, even when doing so unknowingly.

The quest for a well-developed self has hurdles to overcome, many of a psychological nature. Christianity is not a sure road to overcoming this. It depends much on how its faith is understood and expressed. Psychiatrist

Paul W. Pruyser specifies what is needed for religion to offer wellbeing. He writes:

> But if pressed to state one criterion of healthy religion I submit that it lies in the biblical declaration that "the truth shall make you free." .... I regard an enlarged sense of freedom as a sign of psychological, moral, and spiritual health (1991, 65).

This idea was presented earlier in our discussion when raising the question of how much space I feel to have when walking around within myself. What might be the emotional infections I carry within? Is my conscience bothering me and why? Can I freely interact with Jesus, or do I feel some restraint and for what reason? These questions, and others, are the ones to be faced about the level of freedom experienced in soul awareness. Jesus came to set free and make free indeed (John 8:36). It is an area the church should assist in, but mostly it is a matter of personal commitment to a relationship with Christ in private.

The liberation of self will be guided by God's Spirit when so desired. It is a special dynamic. God is ever present within every person through universal love and universal spirit even though the potential of that presence may lay dormant. Meister Eckhart (*c.* 1260-1329) insisted on there being a divine point of connection within every soul. Thomas Merton explains:

> Eckhart speaks of the mystical spark or centre of the soul, the point of contact with God, not as something static or inert, but as a living dynamic "agent." This "agent" makes God live in the soul and the soul in God, and consequently it is in everyone. But in many it has lost its life, through sin, and God is then "dead" to such souls. Yet the Father speaks to such souls in the words of Christ raising from the dead the son of the widow of Naim, and the agent comes back to life, recovering its capacity to "sense" the presence of God by love. This "agent" is the likeness of Christ in the soul; *its innermost self*, the soul's spiritual life in God (2004, 84).

With the whole of creation existing in Christ, it follows that a complete disconnect with Christ is not possible for that would mean non-existence. At the centre of the soul dwells a relational connect with God that cannot be extinguished. The vibrancy of that connection varies. Within a Christian 'the divine spark' may burn brightly depending on how much value is placed on interacting with the Lord. God is love and the ultimate in soul wellbeing is achieved by expressing that. Created in the image of God, people have an exceptional relational potential. A strong and healthy identity is founded on a caring disposition, being relationally open and forgiving, with a proper sense of humility. All of which is an expression of love. When a believer seeks to 'spark brightly' and wilfully aims for that light, the Lord will respond and embrace in mysterious ways in aiding the developmental progress. The spirited soul can be sure of that. Isaiah observed: 'You keep him in perfect peace, whose mind remains on you, because he trusts in you. Trust in the Lord forever, for the Lord God is an everlasting rock' (Isaiah 26:3-4).

Peace of mind in every day is hard to come by. Isaiah's statement is one of possibility and presents a faithful and dependable God. Peace is not a common quality in creation where disintegration and death are ever active. Within the spirit of every living thing the power of sin is operative against that of love. In personhood that battle reaches the level of meaningfulness. The effects of love and sin become qualitatively understood. This is an ability that resides within the human spirit and is central to soul awareness. It determines much.

A positively spirited soul that seeks 'the good' will be one that furthers wellbeing, as would have become clear by now. This positivity exists against the negative and ideally should reign over it. Positive psychology suggest to simply forget about the negative and concentrate on the positive. That approach has attitudinal merit. But the real question is not whether I can be positive, but whether my soul is healthy – not a surface health, but at a deeper level. Some positive, high achievers are narcissists and psychopaths. Soul is a deep water.

It is best to acknowledge that this depth is beyond human ability to sort out. There are two ways in which positive change becomes possible. The first one is consistently seeking the good above the bad, the unselfish rather than selfish, both in attitude and behaviour. Personhood has been so designed that this brings a measure of peace to the self. It is a way towards wellbeing for all. The second way in which to make change possible, and additional to the first, is to invite the Lord into this process. Either way is not an easy road to travel. It is characterised by words like selflessness, self-sacrifice, self-denial and self-examination. The Christian may add that of faith and self-surrender. If the self-giving way seems too hard a path, it is because the benefits are not sufficiently understood;

nor is the help that any person's spirit may draw form Presence when seeking 'the good'. Some people, due to how life has treated them, may be too psychologically damaged to manage this adequately. God will be merciful to them.

Positive change is a central theme in the letters of Apostle Paul. Unlike positive psychology, which is focused on improved ability to cope with life, Paul's approach hits much deeper into the psyche. Like positive psychology, it suggest a change of mind, but of a different kind and being far less egocentric.

> Whatever is true, whatever is honourable, whatever is just, whatever is pure, whatever is lovely, whatever is gracious, if there is any excellence, if there is anything worthy of praise, think about *these* things. (Phil. 4:8)

In Colossians 3:5-17, Paul writes about the transformed walk of the Christian life. It starts with the instruction to put to death, 'what is earthly in you: fornication, impurity, passion, evil desire, and covetousness, which is idolatry.' Many aspects of what that entails follow. Then Paul encourages to put on, 'compassion, kindness, lowliness, meekness and patience,' and exhorts to be forgiving and above all to put on love.

This attitude to life is what Christianity is about, an advice that is frequently forgotten for it demands much. What is insufficiently recognised is that the wellbeing of spirit and soul depends on it far more than on daily prayers. Spirit and soul are nurtured best by a right disposition. There is little that is 'spiritual' about it.

A healthy spirit is basic to a healthy body and mind, and soul awareness thus becomes a better experience. Not just for the individual self but by association for those who are exposed to its relational expressions. There is a fine word in English, not now often used, but once much appreciated by Aristotle and featuring significantly in his philosophy. It is the word 'magnanimity'. It means greatness of soul, that quality of mind which raises a person above all that is mean or unjust. A magnanimous person is a generous person.

Perhaps Micah may have the final word in this chapter on the spirited soul. 'He has showed you, O man, what is good; and what does the Lord require of you but to do justice, and to love kindness, and to walk humbly with your God' (Micah 6:8).

16

Oh My Soul!

Personhood is incredible and in its depth will remain a mystery. Informed comments are helpful, but none must be taken as definitive. Nevertheless, the inquiry into personhood towards better understanding should continue. As may everything else of God's creation be investigated. The sciences are making great headway with amazing discoveries clearly showing the extent of human intelligence.

A Christian approach to knowledge should value the sciences but contains an overriding concern summed up many centuries ago by Anselm's *faith seeking understanding*. It is particularly relevant to when a Christian studies the humanities. AW Tozer commented that the world needs to know before it can have faith, while the Christian needs faith for matters to become known. This comment refers to revelatory insights that will remain hidden unless approached with faith and spiritual intuition.

Tozer observes that, 'faith is an organ of knowledge

that can tell us more about ultimate reality than all the findings of science' (1978, 154). A true understanding of what nature is about is organic and not limited to reason and experimentation. Many insights are ethereal and will not be logically captured. As a painter might show by strangely depicting reality on canvas or a poet in the use of words. Or how God remains diffused in nature.

Our discussion about soul awareness began with a little story called 'Sepia Land' in which the world is shades of brown. It depicts a unity of creation that even though differentiated is undivided. Within that 'brown' creation people exist as an image of God in a reality that originates from the Love of God. Love is the ultimate relational expression and fundamental to the nature of the universe. Everything that exists does so being in relation, and most importantly so with God despite the power of sin being operative.

People are a unity of spirit, body and soul whereby the soul is an awareness derived from the interactions between spirit and body. They find their origin in Presence, a reality that involves universal spirit. Nothing finds reality unless by this spirit, including personhood. The nature of personhood is deep and far greater than a mere biological function, as the sciences would suggest.

Insights into what personhood entails enhances self-understanding and one's identity formation which, when developed with the help of God, can reach its best potential.

By faith God may be understood; a progressive understanding that is a healing process the possibilities of which depend on disposition and making choices. The invitation to choose rightly will always present to soul awareness and a correct response determines how a person's spirit will find its equilibrium in a frantic world. The soul will sense its integration over time, without really knowing how that happens. Personhood cannot ever be sufficiently explained and by nature is everlasting.

With personhood being everlasting might the soul be likewise? It depends on your conception of what the soul is about. I have presented soul as being an awareness that eventuates from the interactions between spirit and body. Once the body dies this interaction will cease and consequently earthly awareness likewise, meaning that soul is no more. As mentioned previously, Ecclesiastes 12:7 states that upon death 'the dust returns to the earth and the spirit returns to God who gave it.' Whether in the New Creation, with everything being clothed in a new body, the idea of 'soul' again is relevant, I cannot know.

What I do know is that surely I will be conscious of my identity.

When people wonder what will happen to their soul upon death, it refers to their essential being and not soul awareness as such. Historically, the terms 'spirit' and 'soul' have been used interchangeably in theology and philosophy, as has been discussed. With Ecclesiastes in mind, I suggest that a person's spirit returns to God as a manifestation of the whole person. That includes all of one's earthly life experiences, the conscious and the unconscious. For how otherwise can my life be evaluated by the Lord in a way meaningful to me? In spirit I may look like my earthly self that will be clothed anew in an imperishable body.

Scripture is clear that there will be an appraisal of a person's earthly life for everyone – questions will be asked. The wisdom of this is with the Lord, who is the personification of Love. How divine Love, caring and embracing, will judge human shortcomings is not something I can know. What I do believe is that when someone has lived as a decent human being the door called Jesus Christ will not close upon them and all will be well. For someone who has succumbed to serious wrongdoing, all is not lost. Christians are not excused from God's appraisal as the judgment seat of God (or

Christ), spoken about by Apostle Paul, makes clear (Rom. 14:10; 2 Cor. 5:10).

Personally, I consider being Christian a privilege; that a divine presence has been bestowed upon me in the way it is. It is an honour that I am able to look after my soul with the help of the Holy Spirit. Heaven is God's business and I have not too fixed an idea about what it involves. God *is* Love and when this Love has its Day in Court, where it evaluates and also divinely loves what is under inspection, then the outcome and its repercussions will be covered in Love! That is sufficient for me.

What matters is how I go about my life, which is an artful engagement – a process of trial and development. A regular, personal evaluation of that process is best, but not to the point of it becoming discouraging. Comments people make about my behaviour I should consider wisely, though perfection is not something I aim for. I will be careful of not becoming my own worst critic. In this difficult task of guarding my soul I will cut myself some slack.

With regard to poetry, in his *Letters to a Young Poet*, Rainer Maria Rilke warns against public opinion, criticism in particular, and explains how art will take its time. He writes beautifully about what true poetry involves and I would think it applies to the flowering of the soul likewise. Rilke deserves to be quoted at length.

> Let me at once make this request: read as little as possible in the way of aesthetics and criticism – it will either be a partisan views, fossilized and made meaningless in its lifeless rigidity, or it will be neat wordplay, where one opinion will triumph one day and the opposite the next. Works of art are infinitely solitary and nothing is less likely to reach them than criticism. Only love can grasp them and hold then and do them justice. – With regard to any such disposition, review or introduction, trust yourself and your instincts; even if you go wrong in your judgment, the natural growth of your inner life will gradually, over time, lead you to your insights. Allow your verdicts their own quiet untroubled development which like all progress must come from deep within and cannot be forced or accelerated. *Everything* must be carried to term before it can be born. To let every impression and the germ of every feeling come to completion inside, in the dark, in the unsayable, the unconscious, in what is unattainable to one's own intellect, and to wait with deep humility and patience for the hour when a new clarity is

> delivered: that alone is to live as an artist, in the understanding and in one's creative work.
>
> These things cannot be measured by time, a year has no meaning, and ten years are nothing. To be an artist means: not to calculate and count; to grow and ripen like a tree which does not hurry the flow of its sap and stands at ease in the spring gales without feeling that no summer may follow. It will come. But it comes only to those who are patient, who are simply there in their vast, quiet tranquillity, as if eternity lay before them. It is a lesson I learn every day amid hardship I am thankful for: *patience* is all! (2013, 18-19).

The artfulness of soul-full living involves like subtleties. Patience is of paramount importance in art which Rilke learned from Sculptor Rodin during his time in Paris. Similarly, I must have confidence in the potential of my soul and patiently persist in its unfolding. God will reveal, inspire and enable.

There is a poem that always deeply touches me and I would like to quote it in ending our discussion. The verses are by one of Spain's greatest poets, St John of the Cross (1542-1591). Based on his visionary understanding, St

John penned a penetrating insight about Christ and the human person (1991, 57/58).

> A lone young shepherd live in pain
> withdrawn from pleasure and contentment,
> his thoughts fixed on a shepherd girl
> *his heart an open wound with love.*
>
> He weeps but not from the wound of love,
> there is no pain in such affliction,
> even though the heart is pierced;
> he weeps knowing he has been forgotten.
>
> That one thought: his shining one
> has forgotten him, is such great pain
> that he bows to brutal handling
> in a foreign land,
> *his heart an open would with love.*
>
> The shepherd says: I pity the one
> who has drawn herself back from my love,
> and does not seek the joy of my presence,
> *though my heart is an open wound with love for her.*

After a long time he climbed a tree,
and spread his shining arms,
and hung by them, and died,
his heart an open wound with love.

Oh My Soul!

REFERENCE LIST

Beck, JR & Demarest, B 2005, *The Human Person in Theology and Psychology*, Kregel, Grand Rapids

Benner, DG 1998, *Care of Souls*, Baker Books, Grand Rapids, Michigan

Brooks, D 2015, *The Road to Character*, Penguin Books

Brueggemann, W 1976, *Living Toward a Vision*, United Church Press, New York

Bryson, B 2020, *The Body*, Penguin, Black Swan edition, UK

Buber, M 1958. *I and Thou*, Charles Scribner's and Sons, NY

Butler-Bowdon T 2007, *50 Psychology Classics*, Nicholas Brealey Publishing, London

Burns, DD 1999, *Feeling Good*, Collins, New York

Descartes, R 1968, *Discourse on Method and the Meditations*, Penguin Books, UK

Delitzsch, F 1966, *A System of Biblical Psychology*, Baker Book House, Grand Rapids

Ellis A & Harper RA 1997, *A Guide To Rational Living*, Melvin Powers Wilshire Book Company, Woodland Hills, CA

Frankfurt, HG 2005, *On Bullshit*, Princeton University Press

French, RM 1982, *The Way of the Pilgrim*, Triangle, SPCK, London

Glenn, PJ 1978, *A Tour of the Summa*, Tan Books and Publishers Rockford, Illinois

Grayling, AC 2019, *The History of Philosophy*, Viking, UK

Grenz, SJ 2001, *The Social God and the Relational Self*, WJK Press, Kentucky

Harrington, JF 2018, *Dangerous Mystic*, Penguin Press, NY
Hildegard of Bingen 2001, *Selected Writings*, Penguin Books
Julian of Norwich 1978, *Showings*, Paulist Press, NY
Jung, CG 1989, *Memories, Dreams, Reflections*, Vintage Books, NY
Kenny, A 2010, *A New History of Western Philosophy*, Clarendon Press, Oxford
Lonergan, B 1972, *Method in Theology*, Herder and Herder, NY
Magee, B 1997, *Confessions of a Philosopher*, Phoenix, London
Merton, T 1968, *Zen and the Birds of Appetite*, A New Directions Book, NY
Merton, T 2004, *The Inner Experience*, HarperSanFrancisco
Norretranders, T 1991, *The User Illusion*, Penguin Books
Pascal, B 1989, *The Mind on Fire*, Hodder and Stoughton, UK
Pinker, S 2015, *How the Mind Works*, Penguin Books
Pruyser, PW 1991, eds. Maloney HN & Spilka B, *Religion in Psychodynamic Perspective*, Oxford University Press, Oxford.
Rahner, K 1964, *The Eternal Year*, Helicon, Baltimore
Rilke, RM 2013, *Letters to a Young Poet*, Penguin
Robson, D 2019, *The Intelligence Trap*, Hodder
Rohr, R & Ebert A 1990, *Discovering The Enneagram*, CollinsDove
Russell, B 2005, *History of Western Philosophy*, Routledge, London
Sehon, S 2005, *Teleological Realism*, The MIT Press, Cambridge, Massachusetts
Seligman, M 2011, *Authentic Happiness*, William Heinemann, Australia

Spinoza, B 2001, *Ethics*, Wordsworth Classics, UK

St John of the Cross, 1988, *The Dark Night of the Soul*, Hodder and Stoughton, London

St John of the Cross, 1991, *The Collected Works*, ICS Publications, Washington

Tozer, AW 1978, *The Best of A.W. Tozer*, Baker Book House, Grand Rapids

Tournier, P 1968, *A Place for You*, SCM Press, London

Trueblood, E 1979, ed. Newby, JR, *An Anthology*, Impact Books, Nashville.

Whitehead, AN 1929, *Process and Reality*, The Free Press, NY

AgapeDeum

Books by Michael J Spyker

Meeting Emma
An introduction to Christian Spirituality in which Emma learns from theologian Joe how to involve God's spirit in everyday living.

The Primacy of Love
How a theological understanding that creation is essentially an expression of God's love leads to a model that explains the dynamics of human relating based on the Trinity.

Julian's Windows
A contemporary love story that contextualises many teachings of medieval mystic Lady Julian of Norwich.

The Language of Love
A love story that encourages wisdom and wellbeing, and seeking an authentic relationship with Jesus Christ.

Science and Spirit
How science and spirit exist is relation and what that means to Christian understanding.

Oh My Soul!
The meaning of soul, the roots of its awareness, and how soul health is helped by a Christian understanding of the dynamics involved.

Drawings and Reflections
52 short reflections on Christian vibrancy with full-colour illustrations by Jeanne Spyker Hardy.

Living Well
The art of making the best of life relationally. Though based on Christian insights this little book is meant for everyone and avoids religious references.

I Am Willing
A story about miracles and more based on the ministry of Dean Knight, who authors this little book with the help of Michael Spyker.

Shalomat
An adventure in which two young people are being chased across Australia while seeking to fulfil a riddle that has global consequences. The story is based on ideas from spirituality and philosophy.

Available at agapedeum.com

www.ingramcontent.com/pod-product-compliance
Lightning Source LLC
Chambersburg PA
CBHW020324010526
44107CB00054B/1971